THE
ENCYCLOPEDIA
of
CANDLEMAKING
TECHNIQUES

THE
ENCYCLOPEDIA
of
CANDLEMAKING
TECHNIQUES

A Step-by-Step Visual Guide

SANDIE LEA

RUNNING PRESS
PHILADELPHIA · LONDON

A QUARTO BOOK
Copyright © 1999 Quarto Inc.

9 8 7 6 5 4 3 2
Digit on the right indicates the number of this printing

Library of Congress Cataloging-in-Publication
Number 98-68456

ISBN 0-7624-0601-1

This book was designed and produced by
Quarto Publishing plc
The Old Brewery
6 Blundell Street
London N7 9BH
Indexer Mary Norris
Project Editor Ulla Weinberg
Copy Editor Sue Wilkinson
Art Editor Sally Bond
Designer Liz Brown
Photographers Pat Aithie, Martin Norris, Rosa Rodrigo,
Paul Forrester, Colin Bowling
Art Director Moira Clinch
Assistant Art Director Penny Cobb
QUAR.EOCT

Manufactured by Bright Arts (Singapore) Pte Ltd
Printed by Leefung-Asco Printers Ltd, China

This book may be ordered by mail from the publisher.
Please include $2.50 for postage and handling.
But try your bookstore first!

Running Press Book Publishers
125 South Twenty-second Street
Philadelphia, Pennsylvania 19103-4399

Visit us on the web!
www.runningpress.com

Contents

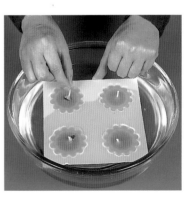

What a feast of pleasures is involved in the craft of candlemaking! Wax is an irresistible material, soft and malleable, and can be molded, sculpted, dipped, and formed into an astonishing range of shapes. It can be colored with luscious dyes and scented with an enormous array of perfumes, from the wild and tangy to the soft and delicate.

The basic techniques of candlemaking are simple and easily learned, but there are many more advanced methods to master, and once acquired your skills can lead you on to your own creations.

▶ Candles look particularly attractive when displayed in groups of assorted sizes. An ornate mirror placed nearby will enhance the sumptuous effect and will also double the amount of light produced.

Introduction

There are many exciting ways to embellish candles. They often incorporate techniques borrowed from other crafts such as painting, stenciling, and carving, and give you the opportunity to apply previously acquired skills, or to learn new ones. Once the candles are made, there follows all the delight of displaying and burning them. The soft glow of candlelight is more popular than ever in today's "high-tech" world. The warm flicker of candle flames can transform a winter evening into a cocoon of atmosphere, while a summer garden at dusk is turned into fairyland by candles twinkling in pots in the trees. Dinner parties have an incomparable sparkle when lit by a crystal water bowl filled with flowers and floating candles, while a scented bath by candlelight is relaxation at its best! Whether you want to enhance a special occasion or simply add richness and pleasure to everyday life, candles can do this for you.

This book will inspire and guide you, whether you are a complete beginner to this fascinating craft or an experienced candlemaker looking for new inspiration. All the main techniques are covered here along with many that are less well known, and the illustrated steps show exactly how each technique is followed. I hope you will find enormous enjoyment in learning new skills or revising old ones, and will be inspired to invent and create techniques of your own.

◀ Impossible to imitate: the simple beauty of a candle flame.

Candlemaking Equipment

The equipment needed for making candles is largely inexpensive and readily available—you may find that you have most of it already in your home!

Candlemaking suppliers sell a wide range of products for making and embellishing candles, but many things can be improvised and suggestions are made throughout this book.

The items listed here are the basic equipment needed for candlemaking. Specific items needed for individual techniques are listed under that technique.

Double boiler This is the safest way to heat wax. Wax begins to vaporize when it is overheated and can then easily catch fire so the safest way to heat it is over water. Alternatively, you can use a saucepan, placed on a trivet and set in a larger pan of boiling water. The water should come halfway up the sides of the saucepan. Alternatively, you could use a large pet-food or oil can.

Trivet Placed in the bottom of pans of water to keep cans of wax off the pan bottom. The trivet only needs to be about ½ in. high. Improvise with a wire cake or grill-rack, or punch some holes in the lid of a paint can.

Dipping can You will need a tall can for dipping or overdipping candles. Proprietary dipping cans are available, or you can improvise with any tall can such as economy-size food cans or metal buckets.

Pouring jug A small jug with a good spout is a great help when pouring wax into molds and for topping up.

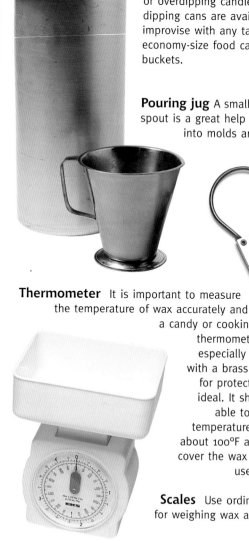

Thermometer It is important to measure the temperature of wax accurately and a candy or cooking thermometer, especially one with a brass back for protection, is ideal. It should be able to measure temperatures between about 100°F and 250°F to cover the wax temperatures used in candlemaking.

Scales Use ordinary kitchen scales for weighing wax and Stearin.

Measuring jug Useful for measuring the amount of water needed to fill a mold so as to calculate the quantity of wax required. For every 3 ½ fl. oz. of water you will need 3 oz. of wax.

Molds There is an enormous variety of commercial molds available made in plastic, metal, glass, latex, and rubber. You can also improvise by using milk cartons, yogurt pots, and custard cups to name a few. See page 38 for a detailed description of all the kinds of molds you can use for candlemaking.

Wicking needles These are used to thread wicks through flexible candle molds. They can also be used for piercing into the cavity during molding and propping a wick on the top of a mold. A large darning needle can be used instead but wicking needles come in larger sizes and are not expensive.

Water bath Use any container that will take the mold. Plastic bowls or large ice cream containers work well.

Weights Used for weighing down a filled rigid mold in a water bath. Old fashioned weights for kitchen scales are ideal, or you can use a large pebble or a jelly jar full of water.

Stirrer You will need to stir the wax when you add dye. Wooden or metal skewers, or knitting needles are ideal for this. You can also use them as a tool to pierce round the wick of molded candles.

Newspaper Spilt wax is a nuisance to clean up so protect your work surface with sheets of newspaper before starting to make candles.

Candlemaking Materials

The materials on these pages covers all that you will need to make candles. Initially, all you will require is wax and wicks, but the more you enjoy the craft, the more you will want to experiment with these different materials.

WAX

There are many different types of wax available and this can be quite bewildering to a beginner. To start with, all you need is a general-purpose paraffin wax, which is sold in craft shops. This is the type of wax that most candles are made with.

Paraffin wax This is either sold in pellet form for easy melting, or in slabs. There are several types that are usually classified according to their melting points:
Low melting point (126°F–132°F). Used for container candles, carved candles, and making modeling wax.
Medium melting point (135°F–145°F). The most useful type of wax that can be used for all molded, dipped, floating, and container candles. Unlabelled wax in craft shops will be this type of wax. A good general-purpose wax, its properties can be adapted for different types of candles by using some of the additives listed.
High melting point (145°F–150°F). Used for specialized candles such as hurricane candles.

Microcrystalline wax This comes in two types:
Hard microcrystalline is used in the proportion 1% with paraffin wax to strengthen candles and make them slower burning. Add approximately 1 teaspoon of melted hard microcrystalline per pound of paraffin wax. Use for hurricane candles, water candles and tapers. It can also be used as a dip to produce beautiful mottled candles (see page 31). It has a high melting point over 200°F, so it should be melted on its own in a small pan over direct heat before adding to melted paraffin wax.

Soft microcrystalline is a low melting point wax that is combined with paraffin wax to make modeling wax (see below). Add 10% (or 1½ oz. microcrystalline to 1 lb. paraffin wax) for container candles to make them stick to the container better.

Dip and carve wax A blend of waxes that is sold specially for making carved candles. It is useful for overdipping candles that will be incised, carved, or hammered because it gives a coating that is less likely to shatter.

Beeswax A beautiful natural wax collected from beehives, beeswax is usually a golden color and smells faintly of honey. It can be used on its own, while only 5–10% added to paraffin wax will improve a candle's color and burning time.
Beeswax sheets are available in both natural and a variety of dyed colors. They are molded with a honeycomb pattern.

Modeling wax This is usually sold pre-colored in bars or pots, and is placed into luke-warm water for 10 minutes to make it malleable. You can also make your own by combining about 10% soft microcrystalline with 90% paraffin wax with a low melting point. Try making small quantities at first to test the result, as waxes vary a lot.

Appliqué wax sheets

These come in a huge range of colors, including metallics. They are extremely thin sheets of wax on a paper backing, which can be cut to shape and then applied to the surface of a candle. You can also buy many different pre-cut motifs.

Candle sand (also called powder wax or bead wax) is a type of granular wax. It can be poured into a container and a primed wick inserted for an instant candle.

Stearin This is added to the wax in the proportion of 10% Stearin to 90% wax (or $1\frac{1}{2}$ oz. Stearin to 1 lb. wax). Stearin aids mold release because it makes the wax shrink on cooling, increases the opacity of candle wax, and enhances dye colors. Do not use Stearin with flexible molds, as it will rot them.

Vybar A proprietary alternative to Stearin for flexible molds. Follow the manufacturers' instructions to work out the necessary amount.

Additives There are various additives sold for candlemaking. Luster Crystals are used to increase strength, enhance color, and improve burning time. Mottling oil will give your candle surface a beautiful snowflake effect. Chalky white (titanium oxide) is a type of dye that gives wax a chalky white opacity. It is used in dip and carve candles and the pour in, pour out technique (see page 48). Pearly white is an additive used to create pastel shades when mixed with wax colors. It also increases opacity, wax strength, and burning time. Follow the manufacturers' instructions as to the use of these products.

Wicks These come in different sizes for different diameter candles, such as $\frac{1}{2}$ in. and 1 in. It is important to choose the correct size of wick for each candle. A wick that is too large will be liable to smoke, and as it provides too much heat, wax may drip down the outside of the candle. A wick that is too small will tend to burn down in a cavity in the center of the candle, although this can be used to advantage for stained glass or other decorated candles.

Plaited (braided) wicks are the general-purpose wicks that are used for most dipped and molded candles.

Wire or paper core wicks are used for votives and container candles, but you can use a well-primed braided wick instead.

Mold release This is brushed on to molds, particularly flexible molds, to make them easier to remove from the candle. Silicone spray or ordinary vegetable oil are alternatives.

Wax glue This is a very sticky type of wax that is used for gluing embellishments to candles. It can either be used as it is, or heated and brushed on.

Wick sustainers (tabs) These are small metal disks with a hole in the center and are used to support wicks in containers.

Candle varnish This is a special shiny varnish available from candlemaking suppliers that can be used as a dip or brushed on. It should not affect the burning of the candle.

Mold sealant Mold sealant is a sticky, putty-like substance used to seal around the wick and wick hole of a mold. You can also use the kneadable sticking compound available from stationers and sold under brand names (Fun Tak or Blu Tak).

Getting Started

This section tells you all you need to know to start making your own candles. Candlemaking has many similarities to cooking: good preparation combined with following the instructions accurately will give you results to be proud of.

Remember that candlemaking is far more an art than a science and while temperatures are important, weight measurements are not critical. If your first attempts are not as you would like, you can simply melt the wax down and try again! The best way to improve is to practice. Candlemaking is not difficult to learn and with each candle you make, you will find yourself becoming more accomplished. The most important thing is to enjoy working with wax, color, and scent to create your own candles!

▼ The basic necessities for making candles are easily found in the home.

THE WORK AREA

Most people who make candles at home find that their kitchen is the ideal work area because heating facilities and a supply of water are the main requirements. However, you can make candles virtually anywhere, so a shed or garage is perfectly adequate if you have a hot plate or camping stove, and a bucket of water.

Before starting, it is wise to cover the work surfaces with newspaper in case of the inevitable spills of wax. Keep a roll of paper towels handy for mopping up wax and wiping out pans. Assemble all the equipment you need before starting so that you do not leave heating wax unattended while fetching things.

SAFETY

You should always follow basic safety precautions when heating wax and making candles:

- Always heat wax in a double boiler, or in a can over water to avoid overheating.
- Use a thermometer to ensure that you do not overheat the wax.
- Never leave wax unattended on a heat source.
- Use oven gloves when handling hot cans.
- Keep a fire blanket nearby and if wax catches fire, turn off the heat source and smother the flames. A wet tea towel can be used in an emergency.
- If you spill wax on your skin, immediately hold it in cold water and peel away the wax gently. Treat as a burn or scald. Wax heated to usual candlemaking temperatures can scald, but it is not usually severe since melted wax is normally well below the temperature of boiling water.
- Keep young children and animals out of your work area while you are dealing with hot wax.

MELTING WAX

First, weigh out the quantity of wax you need. If the wax is in pellet form, it is easy to weigh, but if it is in slab form, you will need to break it up with a hammer and a screwdriver, using the latter as a chisel.

Place the wax in the top section of the double boiler and fill the bottom with boiling water. If you are using a saucepan, place the wax into this and stand the pan, on a trivet, in a larger pan of boiling water. The water should come about halfway up the sides of the saucepan.

Place on a heat source and bring the water up to boiling point, then turn the heat down so that it is kept at a rolling boil. The wax will begin to melt, becoming a clear liquid that looks like water. Continue heating until all the wax has melted. Measure the temperature with your thermometer and heat further until the wax reaches the required temperature.

If you are melting wax for sand candles or for any project that needs a temperature higher than 212°F, melt the wax in a pan over a direct heat. Do not leave the pan unattended and measure the temperature constantly to ensure that the wax does not catch fire.

Water levels The diagrams below show the correct filling levels for the boiling water. Do not overfill or the wax container may begin to float. Also, take care that the water does not boil dry.

Double boiler   **Saucepan and dipping can**

ADDITIVES
If you are using Stearin, it can be melted together with the wax just like wax dye (see page 16 for instructions). Additives that have a higher melting point than wax such as hard microcrystalline should be melted in a small pot over a direct heat before adding them to the melted wax. Scents are usually added last of all, just before dipping or pouring the wax.

Stearin

PRIMING THE WICK
You will need to prime your wicks before use (apart from dipped candles, see page 28). Priming a wick ensures that the wick has wax all through its length so it will burn properly. Cut the length of wick required (these are given in the respective techniques). Dip the wick into some melted wax and leave it for about 30 seconds until it is thoroughly soaked. Remove from the wax, allow to cool for a few seconds, then pull the wick straight and lay it on a piece of foil until it cools and stiffens. It is now ready to be used.

CLEAN-UP TIPS

- NEVER pour melted wax down the sink. It will solidify in the drain and block the sink. Instead, pour leftover wax into a flexible plastic margarine or ice cream tub. When it has set, flex the tub and remove the lump of wax.
- To remove wax from a dipping can, it is best to let the wax cool and solidify on top of the water. You can then cut round the edge of the disk of wax and lift it off the water to store for future use.
- To remove wax from metal surfaces, pour boiling water over the metal. Wax can be scraped off wooden surfaces.
- To remove wax from a carpet, rub the spot with an ice cube and scrape the wax away with a knife. Finally, lay some newspaper on the carpet and iron over it with a hot iron. Any remaining wax will be drawn into the newspaper. This method also works with delicate fabrics, and a hot wash in the washing machine will usually clean wax out of clothes.

Coloring

Part of the delight of making your own candles is coloring them. Dyeing candle wax is easy to do and there are many wonderful colors available. You can mix dyes further to make your own palette of colors.

Color can be the success or failure of a candle. For successful coloring, think carefully about the shape of the candle, its intended use and embellishment, and how it will be displayed. Do you want it to be a bright primary color or a soft pastel, purest white or deepest burgundy? What scents are you planning to use? All these factors should be taken into consideration. If you are combining colors in, for example, chunk or layered candles, you will need to select colors that work well together.

Candles are often made in basic primary colors and although this works well for some, it is a pity not to make use of all the other glorious colors that can be mixed. Try combining red, blue, and a touch of black for a deep burgundy. Or use a small quantity each of orange and yellow with a touch of brown for an amber candle. You only need blue, yellow, and pink (magenta) to be able to make all the colors of the rainbow. Add black and you have all the darker shades at your fingertips as well.

◀ These candles have been made by pouring layers of colored wax into a mold. Each layer is allowed to cool before the next layer is added.

CANDLE DYES

Candle dye usually comes in three different types:

Dye disks or squares These are small blocks of wax that contain concentrated pigments and are easy to use. The quantity of wax they will dye is given on the pack so all you need to do is work out the proportion of the block needed and cut off the necessary amount. The colors are not as stable as powder dyes and this means that adjacent colors (for example, in layered candles) may bleed in time.

Powder dyes These are very strong dyes and only tiny quantities are needed for large amounts of wax. Most professional candlemakers use these dyes.

Candle pigments These strong colors, usually sold as flakes, are used for overdipping only as the pigment does not dissolve in the wax. These cannot be used for making molded candles.

▲ Random cup shapes formed in aluminum foil were used as simple molds for these pretty little colored candles.

CREATING COLORS

Wax dyes come in many beautiful colors and these can be mixed to create further colors of your own. Adding less dye than suggested on the label will provide pastel colors, black added to dyes will give lovely muted shades. Remember that you will not see the true color result until the wax has hardened, so cool a small test sample first.

ADDING DYE TO WAX

Measure the amount of dye you need for the quantity of wax. If you are using Stearin, melt this with the dye before adding the wax. If you are not using Stearin, you can stir the dye into the wax when it is melted. When dipping candles, dye can be melted into the wax when it is floating on the hot water in the dipping can to adjust the color as required. Stir well until all streakiness has dispersed.

Scenting

Scenting your candles adds a glorious extra dimension to candlemaking, and there are dozens of different scents that you can choose from.

When a scented candle burns, the heated wax releases its fragrance into the air to scent the entire room. The variety of special candle scents available is remarkable. There are favorite flower scents such as rose, jasmine, gardenia, and freesia and spicy scents such as cinnamon, clove, and peppermint. Then there are exotic scents such as mango, sandalwood, and patchouli and fantasy scents such as "Meditation" and "Rain." Furthermore, there are scents such as citronella, which discourages insects, and scents for dispersing tobacco smoke.

Choose fragrances to complement the colors and styles of your candles. For example, lemon-scented, pale yellow candles decorated with green appliqué leaves give a luscious effect, as do chocolate-scented, dark brown tapers embellished with gold leaf.

Scents that can be used for candlemaking come in various forms and need to be oil-based so that they will dissolve in wax. Alcohol-based perfumes should not be used.

◄ Add drops of scent to your wax after it has reached the correct temperature and just before you make the candles. This minimizes the likelihood of the scent being spoiled or vaporized by the heat.

Fragrance oils These are scents that are specially made for candlemaking. They are usually synthetic, combine well with the wax, and do not affect the burning properties of the candles. They are available from candle-making suppliers, and are sometimes sold in solid form as scented wax squares. Many varieties are available including blends with exotic names such as "Ocean spray" or "Christmas Spice." Add drops to the melted wax in the proportion given on the bottle.

Fragrance oil

Essential oils These are natural oils that are extracted from flowers and other natural substances. They are usually much more expensive than fragrance oils and may not combine properly with the wax or burn well, so you should test them first. They are very concentrated and only a few drops are needed per pound of wax.

Essential oils

Scented wax beads You can purchase ready-scented wax beads to add to your melted wax. Follow the instructions on the packet to obtain the correct quantities.

Scented wax beads

slices of lemon
and orange

cinnamon sticks

cloves

vanilla pod

fresh herbs

Herbs, flowers, and spices These natural materials can be used in either fresh or dried form to scent wax. Try using lavender flowers, mint leaves, cinnamon sticks, cloves, or fragrant rose petals. Add about a handful of fresh material (or one tablespoon of dried) to 1 lb. of melted wax in the melting pot. Leave to infuse in a pan of simmering water for about 30 minutes, keeping the temperature of the wax at about 170°F. Strain the wax through gauze or a sieve.

lavender

fuschia

rose petals

MAKING TECHNIQUES

You can create candles in an enormous variety of shapes and sizes. This is what makes the craft of candlemaking so fascinating. Once you have mastered one type of candle, there are countless other techniques to try. Some are extremely simple; others are more complex. Most, however, only need a little practice to achieve a professional-looking result.

Carving

This spectacular technique is also called "Dip and Carve," or "Cut and Curl." It uses a combination of dipping, slicing, and twisting the wax to produce stunning candles in a variety of designs.

A molded core candle is dipped repeatedly into different colors of wax, which are then cut and partly peeled away to show the layers underneath. In this example, a star-shaped molded candle is used for the core because its vertical ridges give symmetrical surfaces for carving. The dipping process leaves the candle wax soft and malleable so that it is easy to carve, but it is important to work quickly so that the entire process is completed before the candle has cooled down.

The tools needed for this technique are a simple knife and a potter's wire modeling tool. Both tools need to be extremely sharp to cut the wax cleanly. An apple corer is used for the final trimming of the candle top but you can use the knife instead, although the result will not be as neat.

Dip and carve wax is a blend developed specifically for this technique and is the easiest wax to use. When used for the overdipping, it remains malleable for some time and is less likely to crack. The wax should be dyed with strong colors that do not bleed—either powders or pigments are suitable. The chalky white dye (Titanium dioxide) suggested is a very opaque dye that is particularly suitable for defining the layers in this type of candle. The candles can be overdipped in many beautiful combinations of colors, and the slicing and twisting of the flaps will reveal the internal layers.

You will need to hang the candle from a firm support while you carve and shape it, so use a hook in the ceiling or a solid frame for this. The candle should hang comfortably at eye level.

☞
See also:
Coloring, pages 16–17

YOU WILL NEED

Molded six-point star candle with long wick
Dip and carve wax—clear, chalky white, plum red, dark green—4 oz. of each color
Dipping can for each color
Container with cold water
Meat hook
Sharp knife
Potter's wire loop tool
Gloss candle dip (optional)
Scissors
Apple corer

1 Tie the wick securely to the meat hook. Be sure to tie a double knot that will not slip as the candle will become very heavy with the overdipping.

2 Set up dipping cans for the different wax colors. Holding the core candle by the meat hook, dip it into the red wax and hold it there for 30 seconds to soften it. Lift it out of the wax for about 30 seconds, then dip it into the red wax about five more times to build up a thick layer of red wax.

3 Dip the candle into the white wax next, and immediately dip it briefly into the container of water. This will set the wax on the outside and prevent the candle becoming too warm. Wipe off the excess water with your hand. After this step, alternate every wax dip with a dip into the water.

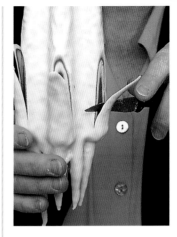

4 Dip the candle about five more times into the white wax to build up a thick layer, then dip into the green wax several times to make a green layer, and finish with another thick layer of white. This will give the candle 25–30 dips in total, and a wax layer of about ½ in. wax will have built up on the core candle. Hang the candle up on a frame or hook.

6 Make a long slice with your knife down one of the protruding ribs of the candle. The cut should be about 1 in. wide and reach from the middle of the candle almost to the base. Repeat this slice on all the ribs around the candle.

7 Bend one of the flaps out and down, curving it over and pressing it on itself at the base. The malleable nature of dip and carve wax allows you to do this without it cracking as long as it is warm enough. Repeat for the other flaps, working swiftly around the candle.

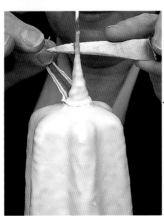

5 Working swiftly before the candle cools down too much to work the wax, trim the wax around the wick. The final trimming around the wick and the trimming of the base will be done after the candle is completed.

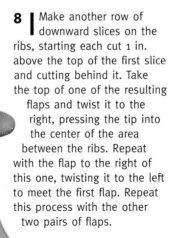

8 Make another row of downward slices on the ribs, starting each cut 1 in. above the top of the first slice and cutting behind it. Take the top of one of the resulting flaps and twist it to the right, pressing the tip into the center of the area between the ribs. Repeat with the flap to the right of this one, twisting it to the left to meet the first flap. Repeat this process with the other two pairs of flaps.

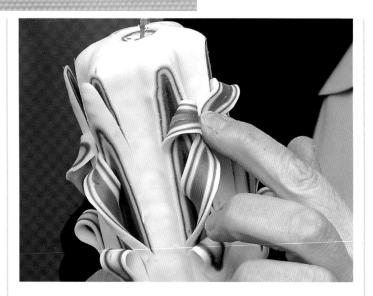

11 To make the candy twists, use the pottery tool to cut a long flap in one of the recessed areas between the bows. Again, the shape of the tool allows you to make a cut in the concave surface.

9 Make a third row of slices, as before, this time starting each cut at the top of the candle, and cutting down to just below the top of the second cut. Bend the flaps inwards in pairs as before, this time curving them downwards, and press them on the center of the lower pairs to make four loop bows.

10 Using the potter's tool, gouge a short flap out of the wax above each bow. The shape of the tool allows you to make a cut into this concave area. Curve the flap down and press it on the center of the bow. Repeat for the other two bow centers.

12 Twist the flap until it is an even spiral all along its length, and then press the top back into place. Provided you have worked quickly enough, the wax should still be malleable. Repeat to make two more candy twists in the remaining spaces between the bows.

13 To trim the base of the candle, grasp it by the drips under the base and cut all round with the knife. Try to cut the base as level as possible, although it can be further trimmed later if it does not stand straight.

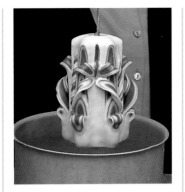

14 Dip the candle into clear dip and carve wax to consolidate all the cuts and flaps and to give it a protective layer. If you want your candle to be shiny, you can dip it into a clear gloss candle dip and allow it to dry for a few minutes. Do not leave it to cool for too long, as you still need it to be soft enough for trimming the top.

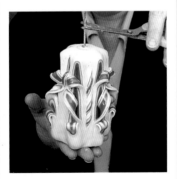

15 Cut the wick with a pair of scissors to release the candle from the meat hook. At this point, you should leave the wick about 1 in. long.

16 Place the apple corer over the wick and center it on the top of the candle. Press the corer straight down into the wax about ¹/₂ in. deep. Slide the corer up and it will remove the plug of wax neatly. Trim the wick to ¹/₂ in. before burning the candle.

▶ The finished candles resemble china ornaments. Apart from the tapers, the flame burns down within a central hollow and illuminates the candles from within. A tea light will make the candle everlasting.

TIP Tapers can be carved in the same way as molded candles and the results resemble beautiful wrought iron curlicues. Because the taper is relatively slim, it is best to carve and twist flaps on only two opposing sides of the candle.

Container Candles

Container candles are great fun to make, and you can have a lot of pleasure choosing suitable containers. There is no limit to the size of these candles, which can be as small as an eggcup, or as large as a bucket!

You can use many different kinds of container for container candles, from small pottery or china bowls to flowerpots, glassware, tin cans, and galvanized buckets. The wick for container candles needs to be either the exact size required so that the level of the candle drops evenly as it burns, or, for larger candles, a smaller size so that the candle burns down in a cavity in the center. See page 12 for advice on selecting wick sizes.

Here are some suggestions for containers, and any safety requirements that may go with them:

CHINA AND POTTERY CONTAINERS These are ideal for candles and need no preparation.

GLASSWARE Candles look beautiful in glass containers because the color of the wax shows through and glows in the flame. Use wax without stearin to enhance this effect. Wineglasses, beer mugs, or recycled jars are all suitable. Cut or engraved glass is particularly attractive, and glassware can be painted, or gilded for further variety. It is advisable to warm glass containers gently in the oven before filling with hot wax to avoid cracking them.

METAL CONTAINERS These range from recycled food tins and cans, to enamelware and galvanized buckets for outdoor candles. As the metal can get very hot, place metal container candles on a protected surface.

TERRACOTTA FLOWERPOTS These are very attractive containers for candles and can be left plain, or decorated with stenciling or painting. You should seal the inside of unglazed pots with a coat of polyurethane, as otherwise the wax will impregnate the pot, which could then catch fire.

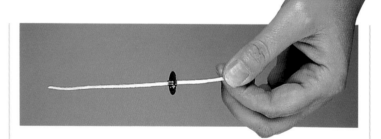

YOU WILL NEED
Container
Primed wick and sustainer
Pliers
Paraffin wax (sufficient amount for container)
Stearin (optional, 10% of wax weight)
Wax dye and scent (optional)
Two small orange sticks

1 Prepare the container and wicking materials. Measure the wick inside your chosen container and cut it a few inches longer than the container's height.

2 Thread the wick through the sustainer, pulling it through until the end of the wick is flush with the bottom of the sustainer. Use pliers to nip the sustainer tube and trap the wick.

3 Place the sustainer and wick centrally in the container and prop the wick with the two orange sticks. You can use a little wax glue to keep the wick sustainer fixed centrally and some mold seal to hold the sticks in place on the rim of the container.

6 If you are using a large container, the wax might sink again and need a third top-up. When the candle is completely cold, remove the sticks and trim the wick to about ½ in.

4 Heat the wax to 160°F, and add dye and scent if required. This low temperature is desirable for pouring so that the wax shrinks as little as possible in the container. Pour the wax up to just under the required level. Be careful not to let the wick move away from the central point.

TIP As container candles do not have to be removed from a mold, there is no need to add Stearin unless you wish to enhance the color of the dye or to create a more opaque candle.

5 Allow the candle to cool completely, then top up with more wax to just above the first level. As the candle will not be removed from the container, it does not matter if some wax goes down the sides. The second pour will partly melt the first pour, so pull the wick straight again and prop upright.

▶ Container candles are a pleasing sight when lit; the flame reflects on the inside of the container to create a warm glow. The small, galvanized bucket contains wax scented with citronella. This is an insect repellent and is ideal for use outdoors.

Dipping

This is the traditional way of making candles to produce beautiful tapers of all sizes and colors. While it is not a difficult technique to master, it does require a little practice.

Dipped candles are made by dipping wicks repeatedly into hot wax until sufficient thickness has built up. Each dip applies a thin layer of wax, and this gives the candles their traditional taper shape. These instructions show how to make hangers for your wicks so that you can dip four candles at any time on one hanger. As dipping candles involves waiting for the wax to cool between dips, it is a good idea to dip several hangers-full of candles in one session as you can then dip in rotation, and allow each group of four to cool while you are dipping the others.

These instructions are for making four 9 in. tapers, which is a good size for beginners. To make longer candles, you will need to use longer wicks, and ensure that the dipping can is tall enough, as the candles should not touch the bottom of the can. If you find the wax layer in the dipping can is becoming thin and patchy as it is being used up you can melt more wax and pour it on top of the water in the dipping can. Remember to match the dye color if you have used colored wax.

YOU WILL NEED

Wire coat hanger or 36 inches of thick wire for each candle hanger
1 in. wick
Cardboard grocery box, at least 12 in. deep and about 11 in. wide
Dipping can, at least 12 in. tall
Boiling water
11 oz. paraffin wax, 135–140°F melting point
Hard microcrystalline wax (optional)
Trivet and large pan
Wax dye and scents (optional)
Scissors

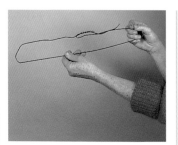

1 To make each wire candle hanger, straighten the coat hanger hook and wind it around the adjacent wire to hold. Bend the coat hanger into a flattened oval, making the long sides of equal length. The candle hangers should be able to rest across the cardboard box so that the wicks hang down inside. This gives you a place to rest the candles between dips and any drips are caught in the bottom of the box.

2 Measure a length of wick, about 9 in. long for 9 in. candles, double it for the two candles and add about 4 in. Cut two wicks of this length.

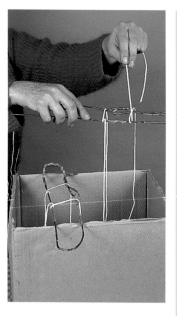

3 Lay one of the lengths of wick over the candle hanger and twist it around one of the wires to hold it in place. Repeat with the second wick, placing it about 2 in. from the first. Do not exceed two pairs of wicks per hanger, or you will find them hard to control while dipping. Lay each hanger across the box top ready for dipping.

☞
Coloring, pages 16–17
Scenting, pages 18–19

4 | Fill the dipping can with boiling water to within 4 in. of the top. Melt the wax and add any color you wish. You can mix in 1% of hard microcrystalline wax at this point. This is not essential, but will make the candles harder and longer burning.

5 | Pour the wax into the dipping can. It will form a floating layer on top of the water. At this point, scents can be added to the wax. Set the dipping can on a trivet in a large pan of just-boiled water on a stove. The water should come about halfway up the sides of the dipping can so that whenever the wax begins to cool while you are dipping, you can safely reheat it.

6 | Lower the wicks on a wick hanger into the melted wax. You will have to shake the hanger gently to ease the wicks in. Allow them to soak up wax for a few seconds, then remove them. Lay the hanger across the box with the wicks dangling inside to cool and stiffen.

7 | Hold the hanger above the dipping can again, and lower the stiffened wicks into the wax, pushing them down and raising them out in one smooth continuous movement. Their stiffness makes them easier to push down. It is important to keep them moving so that the wicks do not remain in the wax for longer than a second or two.

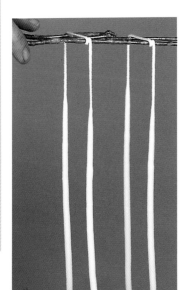

8 | Wait at least 30 seconds to allow the wax to cool slightly, then dip again as before. After a few dips the thickness should begin to build up on the wicks. If it does not build up, the wax is too hot and you must let it cool slightly. If the surface is lumpy, the wax is too cool and needs to be heated a little. The best temperature for dipping is 160–170°F.

TIP Be sure to leave at least 30 seconds between each dip or the bottoms of the candles may sag into a series of bumps. There is no harm leaving the candles longer than 30 seconds, which means that you can dip several hangers of candles in rotation.

9 After about 20 dips the candles will begin to show the familiar taper shape. If they sag or feel wobbly, allow more time for them to cool between dips. As you dip, the wax will be used up and the layer on top of the water will become thinner. You will be able to continue to dip successfully as long as there is a continuous layer.

10 When the candles are about ³/₄ in. thick, trim the bottoms by snipping across them with a pair of scissors. The candles will be quite floppy at this point. Give them a few more dips to finish off. Straighten the candles if necessary and leave them hanging in the box until they are cold.

TIP There are two options when dipping candles: you can either color the dipping wax, or else dip with uncolored wax and overdip the finished candle. Be careful in your use of color because it is easy to over-color. It takes about ten dips to give the true effect so be patient.

GRADED DIPPED CANDLES

Once you have learnt how to dip candles, there are many exciting ways that you can vary them. These candles have been dipped into a second color to give a gently graded look. As wax is relatively translucent, the first color will show through the second where it is thinnest, and will form a third color. Choose your colors carefully as they need to tone.

1 Dip a set of four candles using yellow wax. Add a little red dye to the molten wax in the dipping can. Dip the candles into the wax up to just over half way in one single dip.

2 Dip again but this time to 1 in. below the top of the first dip. Continue making single dips, allowing 30 seconds between and dipping 1 in. lower each time—about four dips in all.

TIP You can make rainbow candles using yellow candles. First dip the bottom half of a candle in blue as above. This will form green where the colors overlap, grading to blue green and then blue at the bottom. Hold the bottom of the candle and dip the top into red. This will combine with the yellow to form orange where they overlap, grading to dark red at the wick. Be sure to leave a yellow section in the center.

OVERDIPPING MOLDED CANDLES

It is often useful to overdip both molded and dipped candles. Any blemishes or irregularities can be covered, poor color improved, or you can simply color a white candle. When dipping molded candles, hold them by the wick and use exactly the same method as for dipping tapers.

For coating a white candle in a colored wax, you may need to overdip several times in order to build up a strong color. If you plunge the candle into cold water immediately after the final wax dip, it will have a shiny surface.

1 Dip a white molded ball candle once into orange wax to give it a subtle warm color. Hold it at an angle and then dip it into blue wax.

2 Allow the candle to cool for a while or your fingers may damage the soft surface of the warm wax when you make the next dip. Dip the candle into blue wax for the second time, but at the opposite angle to the first blue dip.

3 The center egg-shaped candle has been dipped twice into blue for a strong color; the candle on the left has been graded with blue dips over white.

▼ The orange taper shows the effect of graded overdipping, while the blue and white taper is graded at both ends so that the original white appears as a band in the center. The cube and red egg candles have been overdipped in hard microcrystalline wax, which gives a lovely mottled effect.

Dripping

In this technique, wax is dripped upside-down to make a candle that simulates the stalagmites of cave formations. Dripped candles are quite time-consuming to make but the results are beautiful when the candle is lit.

Most people are familiar with the bottle used as a candleholder that is covered in a waterfall of deliberately dripped wax. Dripped wax resembles icicles or stalactites and the results can be very attractive. Here, the wax is dripped over a disc of wax to produce a ring of fragile forms that soar upwards around a pool of blue when the candle is righted. The little icicles of wax glow when the taper is lit.

It takes some time to drip the wax over the disc and build up the wax. To speed up the process it is best to use wax that is almost on the point of setting, to work in a cool environment, and to use a small spoon for many applications.

Hard microcrystalline wax is a useful additive in this technique as it strengthens the wax icicles. As it has a high melting point, the drips form much more quickly with this type of wax and the frosty effect is an added bonus.

YOU WILL NEED
Small dish
Vegetable oil
10 oz. paraffin wax
Hard microcrystalline wax
Blue wax dye
Jelly jar or glass
Large shallow dish to
    catch drips
Spoon and knife
Matches
Small blue taper

☞
Coloring, pages 16–17
Water candles, pages
68–71

1 Oil a small dish and fill it with a layer of 5 oz. of paraffin wax colored with blue wax dye. When set, remove the wax disk from the dish and place it upside-down on a jar. Place the jar in a large shallow dish. Heat the remaining wax with 1% added hard microcrystalline wax (alternatively use pure microcrystalline for a frosted candle). Allow the wax to cool slightly, then start spooning small dribbles all round the edge of the disk, allowing them to drip over the edge to form "icicles" of setting wax.

2 The wax will begin to build up on the disk and run over the edge. If you spoon well back from the edge at first, the wax will have cooled as it reaches the edge and will set into longer drips.

3 Allow the wax to cool for ten minutes between each application. You can speed up the process by placing the candle in the refrigerator, but be careful as it is very fragile.

4 When the drips have built up sufficiently, leave the candle to cool. Carefully lift it off the jar and turn it over. Gouge out a hole in the center of the disk, large enough to take the base of the small taper and about ³⁄₈ inch deep. Heat the base of the taper with a match, let wax drip into the hole, and insert the taper into it.

5 Hold the taper in the hole until it has set firmly, taking care not to knock any of the drips. It is best to choose a taper in a color that tones with the disk: in this example, the taper is dark blue at the base to match the disk and grades to pale blue at the top, which gives an attractive effect.

TIP Instead of adding a taper to the center of the disk, you can pierce a hole in the center with a hot wicking needle or a skewer and insert a primed wick.

▼ Although fragile, these candle bases can last indefinitely. The central taper can be replaced when it has burnt down. The smaller candle has drips made from pure hard microcrystalline wax to give a lovely frosty effect.

Flares

These giant-sized candles are perfect for barbecues and beach parties. Each flare is made on a strong bamboo cane that is driven into the ground to hold the flare upright while it burns.

Outdoor flares will burn for one or two hours with a strong flame that is only extinguished by strong winds. Uncolored wax is used for the inner layers of the candle, but you can use up old wax of any color for this as it will not be visible as the candle burns. For the final dips, try graded dipping to make multicolored or rainbow flares. The flares can also be decorated with dripping.

Another option is to add citronella, or one of the other insect repellent perfumes, to the wax to keep unwelcome visitors away from your barbecue!

Provided that these flares are driven securely into the ground, they will burn perfectly safely, but be careful to keep young children away from them.

YOU WILL NEED
Bamboo cane, 2½ ft. long
Brown paper strip, 2 in. wide, 2½ ft. long
Masking tape
12 oz.–1 lb. paraffin wax
Red wax dye
Primed 3 in. wick
Dipping can, at least 12 in. tall

☞
Dipping, pages 28–31
Dripping (Embellishing Techniques), pages 82–83
Recycling, pages 132–135

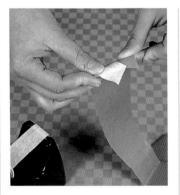

1 Use masking tape to tape the end of the brown paper strip to one end of the cane at an angle. This is to make it easier to twist the strip down the cane.

3 Dip the paper-covered part of the cane into clear paraffin wax that has been heated to about 160°F. Continue to dip until the flare is about 1 in. in diameter.

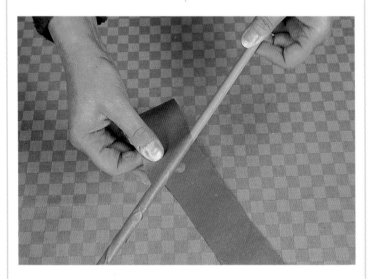

2 Wind the paper strip tightly round the cane, overlapping it slightly so that the wood is completely covered. The paper should cover about half of the cane. Tape again at the end of the strip to secure.

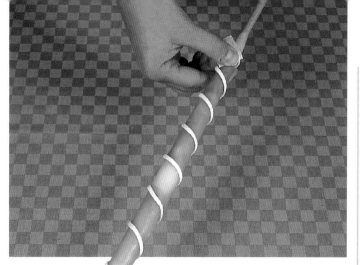

4 Measure and cut a length of primed wick of double the length of the dipped part of the flare. Tape the wick to the top, leaving about ³/₄ in. protruding. Wind the wick all along the dipped length and tape again to secure.

7 Finally, dip the flare a few times into wax colored with wax dye to finish it off. The flare now has a smooth surface and will burn for one to two hours.

▶ The finished flare gives a powerful light. Flares look spectacular at a beach party. Try arranging them in groups of three or four so that they light the way to the sea.

5 Dip the flare again and continue until it is about 1¹/₂ in. in diameter. The thicker you make it, the longer it will burn. The wound wick will slowly become embedded in the dipped wax, and the flare will have a smooth surface.

6 After about 20 dips, the flare is nearly the right thickness. The end of the wick continues to protrude which makes it easier to light the flare.

Floating Candles

Floating candles are eternal favorites for dinner parties where they make a splendid display floating in a suitable bowl along with accessories such as flower petals and leaves. They are usually molded, which is the technique discussed here.

Wax floats on water, so floating candles are simply made with ordinary paraffin wax. The shape of the candle is important, because it needs to be much wider than it is tall in order to float successfully, and not be in danger of capsizing.

You can buy many different molds for floating candles. Some are single molds, and others are multiple molds that will make several small candles at a time. You can also improvise molds by using patty tins and small dishes, or sculpt floating candles from poured wax sheets.

As floating candles are usually quite small, they do not burn as long as larger candles. To extend their burning time, you can add hard microcrystalline wax to the wax.

Some plastic molds, such as the type shown in the sequence below, need to have wick holes drilled in them before use. Alternatively, you can add the wicks after molding.

YOU WILL NEED
Mold
Primed wick
Mold seal
8 oz. paraffin wax
¾ oz. or 2 tbsps. Stearin
Red wax dye
Water bath (optional)
Craft knife, or sharp blade
Pan lined with foil

☞
**Sculpting Flowers, pages 64–65
Ice Bowl Holder, pages 128–129**

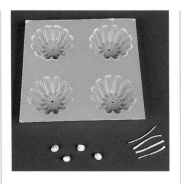

1 Cut the length of primed wick into equal lengths long enough for each mold, with a little extra to tuck under. The wick should be well primed by dipping it into melted wax several times, because otherwise it may absorb water when the candles are floated. Form the mold seal into small balls.

2 Insert a wick through a wick hole, fold the end over at the back, and seal firmly with mold seal. Repeat for the other wick holes.

3 Heat the wax to 180°F with the Stearin and add red wax dye. Fill each mold cavity to the top, using a small, warmed jug so that you can pour accurately. The wicks may fall to one side, but they will be straightened later.

4 Either set the mold aside to cool or place in a water bath where this type of mold will usually float. If you use a water bath to speed setting, be careful that the mold does not tip and fill with water.

5 | When the surface is set, but still soft, pull each wick upright. It is important to do this while the wax is soft because it will sink back after you have moved the wick and leave a smooth result.

6 | Leave the candles to cool completely. As they are small and shallow, the sinking should be minimal and you should not need to top them up. When they are set, remove the mold seal from the bottom of the mold. Straighten the wicks underneath and the candles will drop out of the mold easily.

7 | With a sharp craft knife, or sharp blade, cut off the wick underneath each candle. It needs to be cut flush with the candle base.

TIP | You can wick floating candles while making them, which saves having to make holes in the bottom of the molds. When the candles are nearly cool, insert a length of primed wick. Allow to cool, then trim the wick.

8 | Press the base of each candle on a heated pan lined with foil. This will melt the base slightly and seal the wick. It is important that the wick is thoroughly sealed, as otherwise it will draw up water when the candle is floated. This causes it to splutter, or even go out when it is lit.

▼ Floating candles usually float quite low in the water, so their flames will light up the glass bowl and flowers with a romantic sparkle.

Molding

Molding is a major technique in candlemaking, and molded candles come in a seemingly endless range of shapes and sizes. They are quite easy to make once you have learnt the basic techniques, and molds are available to suit every taste.

Molds for candlemaking come in various materials, and the main ones are covered here. You can also improvise molds from household items such as glasses, bowls, or cans—the only proviso is that the candle must be able to come out of the mold! Most molds are used upside-down so that the top surface of the poured wax becomes the flat base of the candle. A hole is provided in the bottom for threading the wick through, although with flexible molds, you will have to make a hole the first time you use them.

MEASURING THE WAX To calculate how much wax to use, fill the mold with water and measure it. For every 3½ fl. oz. of water, you will need 3 oz. of wax. The best paraffin wax for molding has a medium melting point of 135–140°F. Beeswax can also be used and is often added to paraffin wax to prolong burning time. Even a small percentage of beeswax added to the wax mixture will make it stickier, so use a mold release, or oil the mold.

OTHER ADDITIVES Stearin is a useful additive as it causes the wax to shrink after cooling so that removing the candles from the mold is much easier. It also makes wax more opaque and dye colors more vivid. It is not essential, however: do not use it if you want the wax to remain translucent, such as in hurricane candles, and when adding inclusions. If you omit the Stearin, oil the mold lightly, or use a proprietary mold release. Stearin should not be used for flexible rubber molds as it rots them; use Vybar instead. Candlemaking suppliers sell "Mold sealant," a putty-like substance that seals around the wick hole and the protruding wick very effectively. You can improvise with Fun-Tak (BluTak).

WATER BATH It is not essential to use a water bath, but it speeds up the setting time of the candle. It also gives candles a glossy surface, and makes it easier to remove them from the mold. The water level has to be as high as the poured wax level inside the mold, and the water should not be colder than 40°F or the candle may crack. Alternatively you can leave the mold to set in a cool place, but the setting time will be considerably longer.

RIGID MOLDS

These are the easiest molds for a beginner to use. The most commonly available are clear, or white plastic molds which come in various geometric shapes such as cylinders, cubes, balls, or pyramids. The ball and egg shapes are two-part molds while the others have simple open ends. These molds should not have wax above 180°F poured into them, or they may be damaged. Metal molds are extremely durable and can be poured up to 195°F for excellent results. They are more expensive than plastic molds but will last a long time. Glass molds are fragile, and the shape is limited to cylinders. However, they produce candles with a lovely shiny surface.

YOU WILL NEED
Mold
Primed wick
Support for wick (orange stick, length of wooden barbecue skewer, or wicking needle)
Paraffin wax (sufficient amount for the mold)
Stearin (10% of wax weight)
Mold seal
Wax dye and scent (optional)
Small jug
Paper towels
Water bath and weight (optional)
Scissors or craft knife
Small pan and foil

1 This plastic cone mold comes with its own stand. Start by cutting the primed wick to the height of the mold plus 2–3 in.

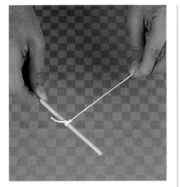

2 Tie the wick to the orange stick. This needs to be long enough to lie across the top of the mold and hold the wick in place.

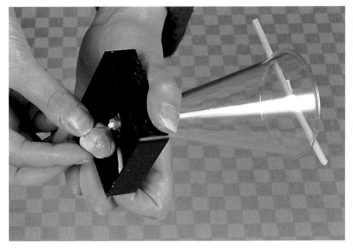

4 Pull the wick tight and apply a generous ball of mold seal to where the wick emerges from the hole. It needs to be secured tightly in place to prevent any wax seeping out of the hole round the wick. Heat the wax, with 10% Stearin added, to about 180–185°F. Add dye and scent, if required.

3 Thread the wick through the hole in the bottom of the mold. It is important to ensure that the wick is precisely in the center of the candle, or the candle will not burn evenly.

5 Protect your work surface to avoid spills, either by setting the mold in a shallow pan or by covering the surface with paper towels. Warm a small jug so that the wax does not cool too much, and fill it with the hot wax. Pour the wax into the mold, filling it to just below the top.

6 Place the mold in a water bath, making sure the water level reaches the top level of the wax. Place a weight on top of the mold to hold it down. Leave the wax to cool until the surface has formed a thick, flexible skin and has sunk in the middle around the wick. The length of time this takes will depend on the size of the candle and the temperature of the water, so check every 10–15 minutes.

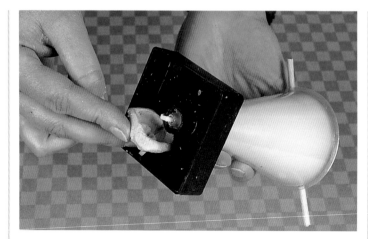

7 | Remove the weight and use a wicking needle or pointed stick to poke several holes around the wick. There will be an air space under the surface and, lower down, some molten wax. This is caused by the wax contracting as it cools, and if this cavity is not filled the candle will not burn properly.

8 | Reheat the remaining wax to 185°F and top up the candle, filling to just below the original level. If you fill any further, the hot wax may run between the set candle and the mold and make it difficult to remove the candle from the mold later.

10 | When the candle is completely cool, remove it from the water bath. With a transparent mold such as this one, you will be able to see that the wax has contracted away from the sides. Pull the mold seal off the bottom.

9 | Put the mold back in the water bath, weight it again, and leave to set. If the wax sinks again in the center, you will need to repeat the topping up procedure. Large candles may need to be topped up several times.

11 | Wiggle the wick to check that it is free, then slide the candle out of the mold. If it will not come out, place it in a refrigerator for a while to cool further; it should then unmold easily.

12 | Cut off the wick at the bottom of the candle as close to the wax as possible, using scissors. Trim the wick at the top to about ¹/₂ in.

▼ Plain molded candles, in bold geometric shapes, have an appealing simplicity. They are also the starting point for many kinds of elaborately decorated candles.

13 | To flatten the base of the candle, heat a small pan and place a sheet of aluminum foil in the bottom. Hold the base of the candle on this for a few seconds so that it melts and flattens to a neat finish.

MOLDING PROBLEMS

Frosty effects or white horizontal lines on the candle surface: The wax was poured too cool.

The candle will not come out of the mold: Place the mold in the refrigerator for a while. If it still will not unmold, place it in hot water for a while to melt it out. You can re-use the wax but you will need to clean the mold. To prevent this happening again:

• Clean the mold thoroughly, wiping it with denatured alcohol.

• Use a thin coat of oil or mold release in the mold.

• Pour the wax hotter so that it contracts more.

• Avoid overfilling when topping up as wax may run down between the set candle and the mold.

Cracks in the candle: Possible causes are: the candle was cooled too quickly; the water in the water bath was too cold; the topping-up wax was too hot (above 195°F).

Bubbles at the base of the candle: The water in the water bath was not high enough.

Tiny pin pricks over candle surface: The wax was poured too hot.

You can overdip a molded candle to cover any surface problems such as those listed above. (See pages 28–31.)

FLEXIBLE MOLDS

Rubber or latex molds come in a large variety of shapes and sizes. As they are flexible, they can be made in very intricate shapes with undercuts and deep relief. Flexible molds will stretch and deteriorate in time. You can buy materials from mold suppliers to make this type of mold yourself.

Virtually any shape can be molded by taking a casting, or painting on layers of latex. Flexible molds are difficult to support when they are full of hot wax. Proprietary mold supports are available for this, but they are not essential.

YOU WILL NEED
Mold
Vegetable oil and
    paintbrush
Primed wick
Support for wick
Wicking needle
Mold seal
Paraffin wax (sufficient
    amount for the mold)
Vybar (optional)
Wax dye and scent
    (optional)
Water bath and mold
    support (optional)
Scissors or craft knife
Liquid detergent
Small pan and foil

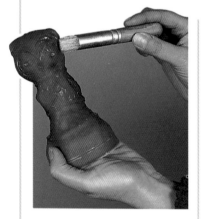

1 | Turn the mold inside out and brush over the inside with oil. Dab off any excess with kitchen paper, as it will spoil the surface of the finished candle.

2 | Tie a knot in one end of the wick and pull it tight around the stick. Thread the other end of the wick through the eye of the wicking needle. Push the needle through the top of the mold, piercing a hole if this is the first time you are using the mold.

3 | Pull the wick straight so that the stick rests across the top of the mold. Seal the hole and wick with mold seal.

4 | Heat wax to 180–185°F, adding Vybar, color, and scent as required. Use a small, prewarmed jug to pour the wax into the mold, as this will make your pouring more accurate. Be careful to support the mold steadily in your hand as you pour—flexible molds can seem to have a mind of their own!

5 | Pinch the mold all over with your fingers to dislodge any air bubbles clinging to the inside. You can see the bubbles if you hold the mold up to a light. Bubbles that are allowed to remain will form pits in the surface of the candle, and can spoil the detail.

6 Place the mold in a water bath. Prop it in a corner and hold it in place against the edge with a large piece of mold seal. For added safety, place a stick across the container to support the mold. Alternatively, you can use a mold support.

7 Leave the mold to cool until the wax has sunk in the center around the wick. Without removing the mold from the water bath, use a needle or skewer to pierce around the wick into the cavity and top up in the same way as for rigid molds on page 40.

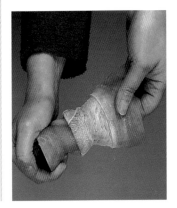

8 Allow the wax to cool until completely hard. Remove the mold by pulling it back onto itself and easing it over the wider parts. If this is difficult, rub liquid detergent on the outside of the mold to help it slip against itself. Trim the wick and flatten the base of the candle in the same way as for the rigid mold candle on page 41.

TIP As with rigid molds, the water bath is optional and you can simply prop the mold in a jug or container that holds it securely until topping up.

▼ This type of mold produces intricate surface textures, as can be seen from the detail on the finished owl candle. The blue and green candles were both made in the same flexible mold. The high relief of the blue candle has been enhanced with some gold paste.

Molding Chunk Candles

Chunk candles are simple molded candles that have chunks of pre-set wax included in them. The brightly colored wax chunks will show up in the candle and give a lively effect.

There are many different options for making these attractive candles. The chunks can be large or small, regular or irregular, of varying sizes, and cut as strips or triangles. If you omit Stearin from the wax, the chunks will be more visible, but you will need to oil the mold, or use mold release.

You can achieve some very interesting effects with chunk candles if you cut out the chunks using a shaped cutter as for wax appliqué. Another idea is to use colored wax for the pouring wax—it will give a wonderfully colorful candle, especially if the chunks are in strong, contrasting colors. To make a candle with a marbled effect, splash the chunks with dribbles of strong dye before pouring the wax: When the hot wax is poured over the chunks, the dye will flow into it to make wonderful swirls around the chunks.

YOU WILL NEED
Shallow container, or pan
Paraffin wax (sufficient
    amount for the mold)
Stearin (10% of wax weight)
Wax dye—green and
    yellow
Heavy-duty craft knife
Rigid mold
Primed wick
Support for wick
Mold seal
Water bath (optional)

☞
Coloring, pages 16–17
Appliqué, pages 74–77

1 The container used here is a waxed paper dish, which allows the cooled wax to be unmolded fairly easily. You could also use a plastic margarine tub, a cake tin, or an ice cube tray. If your container is metal, oil it lightly with vegetable oil.

2 Melt some wax and add Stearin and dye. Pour a shallow layer of the melted wax mixture, about $3/8$ in. deep, into the container. Repeat with another container for a second color if you wish.

3 Leave the wax to set until it is no longer liquid, but still pliable. If it becomes too hard it will be difficult to cut into chunks, but it needs to be set enough for the chunks to hold their shape. Remove the slab from the container.

4 Using a heavy-duty craft knife cut the wax into $3/8$ in. cubes. The wax should cut quite easily, but work quickly so that it does not become too hard. Repeat for the other color if used.

5 | Wick up a mold as shown for the basic rigid mold on pages 38–39. Fill the mold with the wax chunks, combining the colors to make an attractive mixture.

7 | Follow the instructions on pages 39–41 for cooling the candle, topping up the wax, removing from the mold, and flattening the base.

▼ When chunk candles are lit, the glow from the flame lights up the plain wax, making the chunks inside the candle more visible. The orange candle includes orange and yellow chunks.

6 | Heat some clear wax with Stearin to 185–190°F. The wax needs to be hot, as the cold chunks will cool it as it is poured. Also, the hot temperature will cause the chunks to merge slightly into the surrounding wax, and will give the candle a shiny finish.

Molding Hurricane Candles

Hurricane candles are basically shells of wax inside which a small candle is burned. They are called "hurricane" candles because the shell protects the flame from drafts (or hurricanes!).

Hurricane candles are usually made with translucent wax that is decorated in some way, and the flame within lights up the shell. Here, fall leaves are used to great effect, but you can use any other type of inclusion you wish.

In the technique shown here, two bowls are used for the mold so that the inclusions can be trapped between them. You can also make hurricane candles by filling a large mold with hot wax and pouring out the molten center after the sides have hardened. The latter method requires much more wax, and means that you cannot use inclusions, although many other forms of embellishing are possible. Alternatively, you can purchase a proprietary hurricane candle mold that involves using a central section to trap inclusions in the outer shell.

YOU WILL NEED
Two bowls (one about 6 in., the other small enough to fit inside, leaving a ½ in. gap all round)
Vegetable oil and a brush
1 lb. paraffin wax
1 tsp. hard microcrystalline wax
Preserved fall leaves
Funnel
Water bath (optional)
Small pan
Foil

☞
Container candles, pages 26–27
Inclusions, pages 94–95

1 Oil the inside of the large bowl. A plastic bowl is used here as the candle can be removed more easily from the flexible plastic.

2 Melt the paraffin wax and add the pre-melted hard microcrystalline wax (see page 11). Pour about ½ in. into the bottom of the large bowl and leave until it is hard.

3 Brush the outside of the smaller bowl with oil, and stand it centrally inside the large bowl on the layer of set wax. If it slips, use a little wax glue to hold it in place.

4 Push the leaves down into the space between the two bowls, overlapping them slightly so that they will show through as attractive silhouettes when the candle is lit. You can use colorful leaves that have not been preserved if they are dry. They will last a surprisingly long time, as the wax itself will preserve them. Alternatively, use silk flowers or herbs.

5 Fill the inner bowl with cold water. This will weigh it down when the space is filled with wax, and will help to cool the candle. Heat the wax mixture again to 180°F and, using a jug and a funnel, fill the space between the two bowls. You may need to push the leaves down with a stick if they float up.

7 Heat a small pan and line it with a piece of foil. Hold the candle shell upside-down on the foil to melt, and smooth its upper edge. Place a votive candle inside the shell.

TIP Once the basic shell is made, you can either burn a votive candle inside, or fill the center with a 1 in. wick and wax as though it was a container candle. Place the candle shell back inside the larger bowl to do this. When the wick is lit, it will burn down inside the outer shell and shine through it.

▼ When the votive candle inside the hurricane candle is lit, the whole shell glows and the leaves inside the wax form beautiful, translucent shadows.

6 Place the two bowls in a water bath, or leave to stand in a cool place until the wax is set. You will find that a cavity develops inside the wax shell. Make holes all round the top of the shell and top off in the same manner as the rigid mold candle on page 40. When the wax is completely hard, pour the water out of the small bowl and flex the larger bowl so that you can remove the shell. Ease the small bowl out of the middle.

Molding Pour in, Pour out Candles

This is an attractive technique that is used to enhance high-relief candles. Darker wax is visible through an outer coating of white wax, which gives the candles an ethereal quality.

This technique involves pouring white wax into a flexible or rigid mold. When a thin layer has cooled all over the inside of the mold, pour it out again and pour in a dark color wax. This gives a lovely result when used with deeply cut molds because it accentuates the contours of the candle and produces an attractive two-tone effect. Uncolored wax, made opaque by the addition of Vybar, is usually used for the first pour, but you could use any light color. The flexible mold used in the following sequence is of a firtree and the result suggests a covering of snow over dark green branches.

YOU WILL NEED
Flexible mold, oiled, wicked, and sealed
Paraffin wax (sufficient amount for the mold)
Vybar (optional)
Water bath
Spare plastic container
Green wax dye
Scissors or sharp craft knife
Small pan and foil

1 | Heat the wax and Vybar to 175–180°F and pour into a warm jug. Holding the mold upright in your hand, fill it with the hot wax. Pinch the mold to remove any air bubbles.

2 | Place the mold in a water bath so that the water is level with the top of the wax and hold for 90 seconds. A thin skin of set wax will form on the sides of the mold while the wax in the center remains melted.

3 | Remove the mold from the water and tip the molten wax out of the mold into a spare plastic container. You can easily remove the wax when it has set.

4 | Fill the mold again, this time with wax colored with green wax dye and heated to the same temperature. Quickly place the mold in the water bath, so that the green wax does not begin to melt the white wax.

5 | Prop the mold if necessary. This particular mold floats at just the right level, so there is no need to prop it. Leave until partially cool and then top up. Leave until completely cooled.

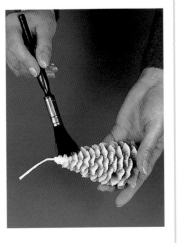

6 Cut the wick off flush with the wax with scissors, or use a craft knife if the scissors will not reach. Remove the stick and any excess wick.

▼ The finished candle shows how successfully the outer layer of wax blends into the inner pour of dark green wax. This makes a lovely winter festival candle, especially when grouped together with other fir tree candles.

7 Remove the candle from the mold, easing the latter over the wider parts. Be careful not to break off any of the wax detail. You can rub the outside of the mold with liquid detergent to make it slip against itself more easily as you fold it back to remove the candle.

8 Brush over the candle with a large, soft paintbrush to remove any loose bits of wax. Finally, trim the wick to about $1/2$ in. Flatten the base of the candle by holding it on a piece of foil that has been placed in the bottom of a heated pan.

Plaiting (Braiding)

Simple plaited candles have a timeless country appeal that conjures up images of corn dollies, homemade bread, and gingham tablecloths. They look particularly good displayed in simple pottery or wooden candleholders.

These instructions show how to plait three simple tapers, but there are many variations of this type of candle. Jewish candlemakers have developed the technique into an art form, using numerous thin tapers. These composite plaits are difficult to master but you can achieve attractive results with simpler techniques: two tapers can be twisted together into a simple rope; or you can use candles in several different colors, candles of differing thicknesses, and even graded dipped candles.

The candles used need to be newly dipped and warm right through so that they will be pliable enough to plait. You can also use previously dipped candles but you will need to warm them first: heat some water to about 125°F and place the tapers in this for at least 15 minutes. Another way of warming candles is to place them in a preheated oven at 200°F on a baking sheet, but check frequently that they are not melting.

YOU WILL NEED
Three freshly dipped tapers, no more than ½ in. thick, made with a ½ in. or smaller wick
Board to work on
Dipping can with matching wax for finishing (optional)

1 You will need to work quickly so that the candles do not cool down and begin to stiffen and crack. Arrange them on a board in a row with the bases together. Working from the bottom of the candles, plait towards the tapered ends, keeping the plait as even as possible and squeezing the candles together as you work.

2 When you reach the tops, squeeze them together into a fine point. Squeeze the bottoms together firmly so that they have a circular cross-section that will fit into a candleholder.

3 If the tops of the candles crumble slightly around the wicks during plaiting, dip them into matching hot wax to consolidate and neaten them. Trim the wicks to ½ in.

TIP Dip the tapers for plaited candles with wicks that are one size smaller than normal, or else the combined wicks will be too large and cause an excessive flame when the plaited candle is lit.

▶ These candles are most entertaining when lit because the flames combine and separate as the candle burns down.

Rolling Beeswax Sheets

One of the simplest ways of making candles is to roll a sheet of wax around a wick. Two methods are covered here: rolling purchased beeswax sheets and rolling sheets of wax that you have poured yourself.

Beeswax sheets have an impressed texture that simulates a honeycomb, and this gives rolled beeswax candles a very distinctive look. The sheets are available in many colors including the beautiful natural golden color. Beeswax is relatively expensive, but has a wonderful soft texture and a delicious smell with a hint of honey that is given off as you handle the wax or burn the candles.

The sheets can be rolled in various ways to give many different shapes of candle from simple pillar candles to tapered and beehive-shaped candles. As these techniques involve no heating, they are particularly suitable for children. You can even buy small plastic bee pins from beekeeper's suppliers to attach to your beeswax candles. These should be removed before burning.

You can also use sheets of beeswax for embellishing candles in a variety of ways, including wrapping them around molded candles or using cutout shapes for appliqué.

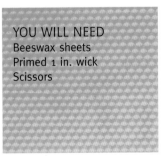

YOU WILL NEED
Beeswax sheets
Primed 1 in. wick
Scissors

☞
Appliqué, pages 74–77
Wrapping, pages
114–115

SIMPLE ROLLED BEESWAX CANDLE

1 Trim the primed wick to the width of the beeswax sheet plus about 3/4 in. Try to work in a warm room when rolling beeswax as the sheets will be more pliable. In cold climates, it is best to keep the sheets at room temperature for 24 hours before use to let them become pliable. They can also be warmed gently with a hair drier.

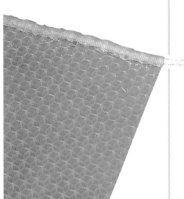

3 Roll the sheet over the wick to encase it tightly, then roll the sheet around the wick four more times, keeping it very tight at this point. If you allow air holes between the rolls, the candle will not burn successfully.

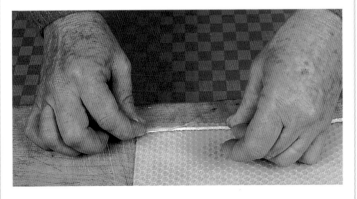

2 Lay the wick along one edge of the sheet and fold this over it tightly. Working along the edge from one side to the other, press it down firmly to cover the wick—the stiffness of the primed wick will make this easier. Make small indents at regular intervals along the wax edge with your nail to secure it and tuck the wick under the edge.

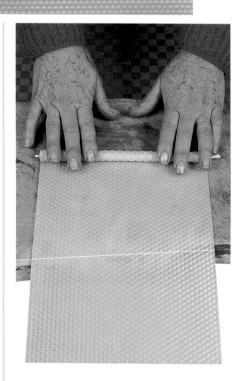

4 Now simply roll up to the other edge of the sheet. Keep it fairly tight and the edges aligned as much as possible for a straight top and bottom to the candle. If you find you are not rolling straight, simply unroll the sheet and start again.

TIP To make a thicker candle, join on a second sheet by butting it onto the end of the first sheet. Pinch along the join with your nail to secure, then continue rolling and finish as above.

5 When the sheet is fully rolled up, work along the join with your thumbnail, nipping it together at regular intervals of about ³/₈ in. Trim the wick to about ¹/₂ in. As a final effect, dip the tip of the candle in melted beeswax to finish it off.

TAPERED ROLLED BEESWAX CANDLE

When a beeswax sheet is cut diagonally into a triangle and rolled up, the result is a tapered candle. The final shape depends on the gradient of the angle cut.

1 Lay the ruler diagonally across the beeswax sheet and offset it from each corner by about ¹/₂ in. Cut the sheet diagonally into two triangles along the ruler edge using a sharp knife. You can make a candle from each triangle.

TIP You can use this technique to make two-color rolled candles. Cut equal sized triangles of two different colored sheets, and trim one along the diagonal edge so that it is ¹/₂ in. smaller than the other. Put the larger sheet on top of the smaller one, aligning the straight edges, and roll up as before. The two colors will be visible in the spiral.

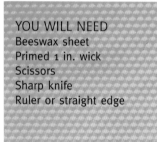

YOU WILL NEED
Beeswax sheet
Primed 1 in. wick
Scissors
Sharp knife
Ruler or straight edge

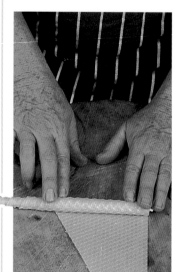

2 Lay the wick along the short edge of one triangle and fold the edge over the wick tightly, using your nail to secure. Roll the candle up, keeping it aligned along the straight edge. The diagonal edge will form the tapered shape as you roll. Finish the candle by nipping with your nail along the tapered edge at regular intervals to secure.

BEEHIVE ROLLED BEESWAX CANDLE

This is a variation on the tapered candle, but it uses three sheets of wax cut at a very shallow angle in order to create the low, chunky dome of the beehive.

YOU WILL NEED
Three beeswax sheets
Primed 1 in. wick
Scissors
Sharp knife
Long ruler or straight edge

▼ This picture shows the finished beehive, the tapered, and the simple rolled beeswax candle. The white-topped candle is a white molded candle with a sheet of beeswax wrapped around it. All the candles are made with natural colored sheets, but you could use any of the many colors available.

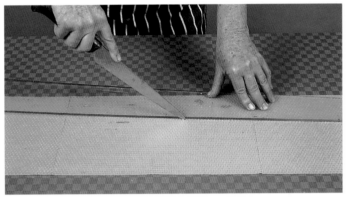

1 Lay the three sheets edge to edge and use the knife and ruler to cut across all three sheets at a very shallow angle, as shown. The widest end needs to be about 3 in. long and the narrow end about 1 in. long, depending on how domed you want the candle to be. Eight inches from the widest end, do not continue the angle but cut straight across to the end.

2 Starting at the widest cut end, roll the wick up as before. When you reach the end of the first sheet, add on the second, butting the edges and pinching along the join with your nail to secure. Continue rolling, adding in the third sheet and finishing in the same way.

Rolling Poured Sheets

It is not difficult to pour your own sheets of wax for rolling candles, and the resulting tapers are slim and elegant.

Dip and carve wax is used for this technique, as it remains soft and workable for longer than other types of wax. Alternatively, you can use a paraffin wax with a low melting point.

This technique uses a smooth board for pouring the wax, in the same way as the sculpting techniques demonstrated in this book. As you will need a large sheet of wax, it is a good idea to glue two strips of $1/16$ in. thick wood to the edges of the board to prevent the wax from flowing over the ends while you pour.

Once you have mastered this technique, there are several ways that you can give variety to these beautiful candles. Try pouring wax sheets of two different colors, then pressing them together before rolling: where the candle is flared out in a spiral, the inside color will be visible. Another attractive embellishment is to tip the edge of the flared spiral with gold or silver paint.

YOU WILL NEED
Vegetable oil
Smooth board or work surface with wooden strips glued to ends
6 oz. dip and carve wax
Blue wax dye
Sharp craft knife
Primed wick, slightly longer than the length of the candle

☞
Sculpting, pages 60–65

1 Lightly oil the board. Heat the wax with the dye until melted, and pour a sheet of wax between the wooden strips. Move the pan slowly over the board as you pour in order to get an even covering. Allow the wax sheet to cool until the surface is set and the edges, when lifted, are still soft and flexible.

2 Working quickly so that the wax does not become too cool, cut out a right-angled triangle with the craft knife. Remove all the wax from around the triangle, and ease it upwards to free it from the board.

3 Lay the primed wick just inside the longer straight edge of the triangle and bend the edge over it tightly, pressing it down to fix the wick inside. Make sure that the wick is tightly encased.

4 Roll the candle up tightly, keeping the roll aligned along the short edge of the triangle, which will be the candle base.

5 Pinch the spiral edge of the candle all along to thin it, and ease it out away from the body of the candle into a slight wing that spirals all the way up the candle.

6 Use a sharp knife to trim the base of the candle, cutting through the wick with scissors if necessary. Be careful not to flatten the spiral edge when you do this. You can use a hair drier to soften the wax at any point in order to adjust the shape of the candle.

7 Hang the candle up by the wick to cool for a few moments, as the spiral will be flattened if it is laid down or could sag into a curved shape.

▶ These candles will burn well provided that they have been tightly rolled around the wick. If the candle base is difficult to fit into a candleholder, hold it in hot water for a few minutes to soften it, then press it into the holder.

Sand Candles

A hole molded in damp sand and filled with hot wax and a wick, is all that is used to make these beautiful, natural candles. Choose soft, muted colors for dyeing the wax to enhance the natural look.

Sand candles can be made in almost any shape and size. All you need is a bucket of damp sand, a wick, and wax. When the hot wax is poured into a hole formed in the sand, the outer layer combines with the sand to form a thick crust when the wax cools. Any type of sand is suitable; use coarse builders' sand for a rough texture or fine silver sand for a more delicate result. You can incorporate pebbles or gravel into the sand too.

Virtually any container can be used for the sand but a plastic bucket or bowl is ideal. The container needs to be large enough to hold the candle comfortably with room for you to get your hands round the edge when removing the candle. If your container is large enough, you can make several sand candles at a time.

The shape of the former used to create the hole in the sand is also infinitely variable. You can use a log of wood, a glass jar, a shallow bowl or simply your hands to make freeform shapes.

☞
**Safety, page 14
Molded candles, pages
38–49**

YOU WILL NEED
Bucket
Sand
Glass or jar as a former,
    about 4 in. diameter, 6
    in. tall
Bowl and spoon
1 lb., 3 oz. paraffin wax—
    medium to high melting
    point
Knife
Primed 1 in. wick
Blue wax dye and scent
    (optional)
Stick or candle hanger
Blow torch (optional)

SAFETY
Wax for making sand candles has to be heated to higher temperatures than is possible with a double-boiler, which will only allow wax to reach the temperature of boiling water or 212°F. You have to be careful when heating the wax over a direct heat source as it can very quickly overheat and ignite. Watch over the pan the entire time and use a thermometer.

1 Fill the bucket with sand, adding enough water to make it slightly damp. To test, squeeze some sand in your hand, then open your fingers: the sand should hold its shape. If it leaves a muddy residue it is too wet and should have dry sand added; if it collapses, it is too dry and needs more water.

2 Scoop out a hole in the sand roughly the size of the shape you are using as a former, in this example a jar. You should not make the mold deeper than it is wide or the candle will be too tall and therefore unstable.

3 Press the former into the hole and pack sand around it firmly. Keep the surface of the sand level, smoothing it around the sides of the former to ensure a neat top to the hole.

4 Carefully remove the former from the sand, taking care to disturb the sand as little as possible. If the sand tumbles into the hole, it is probably not wet enough and needs further damping. Measure the depth of the hole and cut the wick to about twice this length.

6 Pour the wax into the mold over the back of a spoon so that the stream of wax does not disturb the sand. Fill the mold completely with wax—it will bubble fiercely as the wax hits the cool, damp sand.

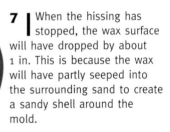

7 When the hissing has stopped, the wax surface will have dropped by about 1 in. This is because the wax will have partly seeped into the surrounding sand to create a sandy shell around the mold.

9 Puncture the center of the set candle surface twice with a knife in the shape of a cross, as this will help you to center the wick. Be careful not to puncture too deep into the candle and disturb the bottom.

5 Use the back of a spoon to smooth the inside of the hole, pressing the sand outwards to firm it. Using a saucepan over a direct heat, carefully heat 1 lb. of wax until it is melted. Continue heating until the temperature reaches 275°F. Do not add any dye or scent at this point as the high temperature may spoil them.

8 Top up with more hot wax to the surface of the mold. Leave the bucket in a cool place until the wax is partially set and the surface has sunk a little. The length of time needed depends on the ambient temperature, so be sure to check the candle at regular intervals.

12 Heat 2–3 oz. of wax to 170°F, this time in a double-boiler for safety, and add blue wax dye. Top up the candle with blue wax, making sure that the wick is still propped on the candle hanger to keep it straight.

14 Scrape off the surplus waxy sand with a sharp knife or a spoon. You will need to remove anything that is loose, scraping back to a smooth layer where the sand is consolidated by wax. Trim the base level with a knife.

10 Insert the primed wick into the center of the cross, pushing it straight down to the bottom of the mold. It will fall to one side but it will be straightened later. Leave the candle to set again.

11 When the wax is nearly hard and the surface has sunk further, pull the wick straight and prop it over a candle hanger or stick, bending the stiff wick over it to hold it in place.

13 Leave the candle to set until it is cool. This can take up to five hours for a large candle. To remove the candle from the sand, first lift off any loose wax lying on top of the sand. Gently dig out the candle and brush off all the loose sand.

15 Use the knife to trim the top edge of the candle until it is level with the surface of the wax and then refine it into a neat edge. Trim the wick to about 1/2 in. long.

▼ VARIATION
Agate candle
The larger candle has an agate inset in its side. As this candle burns down, the candlelight will shine through the translucent agate. To make this type of sand candle, dip a slice of agate into wax several times. Form a mold hole in damp sand, flatten one side, and press the agate into it.

Continue as for the normal sand candle. Remove the finished candle from the sand, peel the wax coating off the agate, and neaten the edge around it.

16 To seal the surface, you can run a blow torch, set to a low flame, all over the sand areas in a waving motion, keeping the flame moving. This will draw wax to the surface and consolidate the outer layer of sand, which will darken. Unless your hand is very steady, it is safer to place the candle on a cookie sheet. Wear clear goggles. Work a section at a time, and when the surface has cooled, pat it all over with your hand to smooth it further.

▶ Using a 1 in. wick for a sand candle of 4 in. diameter means that the flame will burn down in a cavity in the center. Later, you can place a tea light inside the cavity so that the candle becomes everlasting.

Sculpting

Candle wax can be sculpted, as well

as being dipped, rolled, and molded—

a truly versatile medium! The

following sculpting techniques use

poured sheets of wax, but you could also

sculpt with ready-made modeling wax.

The best wax for sculpting with poured sheets is dip and carve, a blend of waxes made for making candles of that name. It has a low melting point and stays malleable longer than ordinary paraffin wax. If you cannot find dip and carve wax, use paraffin wax with a low melting point.

For the following techniques you will need a smooth board on which to pour the wax before cutting and shaping it. A wooden board is the best kind as it retains the heat better than marble or glass, or use one with a smooth covering such as Melamine. If you oil the board lightly, it is easier to lift off the poured sheets of wax when they are still in a malleable state. Take care not to use too much oil or the wax sheets will not adhere to the sculpture.

After you have produced a sheet of poured wax, you will need to clean the board by scraping up the remnants of wax. They can then be put back into the wax pot and heated again.

Even with a wooden board, it is a matter of working against time to keep the wax soft enough to work. Try using a hair drier to warm the sheets of wax if you find that they cool too quickly.

SCULPTING FIGURES

This delightful little wizard is made by sculpting sheets of wax over a cone candle base. The design could be adapted to make other figures, such as an angel, or witch. Melt the different colors of wax in small containers and keep them warm together in a pan of boiling water until needed.

☞
Rolling Poured Sheets, pages 54–55

1 Oil the board very sparingly. Melt 2 oz. of uncolored dip and carve wax. Using the jug, pour the wax on the board to make a thin sheet. The temperature of the wax is not important—it just needs to be melted so that it will pour.

2 Leave the wax to cool until it has set into a flexible sheet. Pull up a corner to test it: The surface should be set, but the sheet must still be soft enough to bend easily. Using the craft knife, cut out two rectangles, each 1 in. by 2 in. Use the palette knife to ease the pieces off the board.

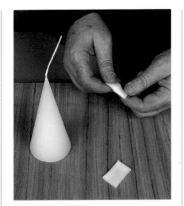

3 | With the wax pieces still warm and malleable, fold each in half lengthways and shape into rough oblongs for the arms.

5 | Pour the purple wax out on the board and cut out the shape of the wizard's gown. If you are unsure about the shape, make a template in paper first and wrap it around the body, adjusting it until you find the correct shape. Use the template for cutting out the wax.

7 | Pour another sheet of purple wax and cut two wedge-shaped pieces. Fold each in half and open out the broad end to suggest the open end of a sleeve. Press onto the body over the arm shapes, using wax glue to help the wax to stick. Cut a long strip of wax to go down the front of the cloak and a shorter strip for the collar. Apply both to the candle, using wax glue to attach them.

4 | Paint some melted wax glue on the inside of each arm with a paintbrush. Press the arms on the sides of the cone candle, about half-way up as shown.

6 | Wrap the cloak around the wizard's body. Trim the base of the cloak and bring it round to meet at the front, trimming it to fit. You will need to work quickly so that the wax stays warm enough to adhere to the body.

8 | Dip the wizard into clear wax, heated to about 170°F, as far as the neckline. This will consolidate all the applied pieces, and cover any fingerprints or rough areas.

9 Pour out a sheet of pale pink wax for the face and hands. Cut out an oval for the face and, using wax glue, press it on above the neckline. For the right hand, cut a square of pink wax, fold it in half, and shape it into a teardrop. Insert the pointed end into a sleeve, using wax glue to hold it.

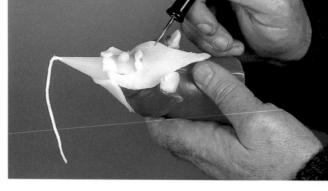

12 Use a wood burner to melt lines of texture into the hair and beard. Alternatively you can use a needle heated over a tea light, but do not put the needle directly into the flame or it will go black, and soil the sculpture.

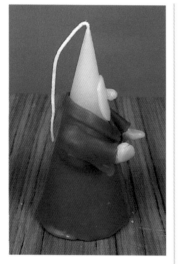

10 Make the left hand in the same way as the right, but shape it flatter so that it can hold the marble. Form a small teardrop for the nose, cut a hole in the center of the face, and insert the point of the teardrop, using wax glue to hold.

11 Pour a sheet of uncolored wax and cut out the beard, the moustache, the eyebrows, and a rectangle for the hair. Pinch the edges of each piece to thin it, and apply using wax glue, shaping it to fit the head. The hair is pressed on right round the back of the head.

13 Press bug eyes onto the face, using wax glue to attach them. Alternatively, you can use small cutout paper eyes. If using plastic bug eyes, remove them before burning the candle.

16 Use wax glue to attach a marble and a stick to the wizard's hands. Cut thin strips from a silver wax appliqué sheet with a craft knife and press them on around the base, sleeves and front of the cloak, and around the hat (alternatively, paint the lines on with silver paint). Glue a star sequin to the front of the hat.

14 For the hat, pour a small sheet of purple wax, and cut out a circle for the hat brim, using a jar or glass as a guide, and a cone shape for the hat crown. Cut a smaller circle out of the center of the brim. Curve the cone into a pointed hat crown, pressing the edges together, and flare out the bottom. Drop the brim over the crown, and pinch the brim and crown together where they meet.

15 Dip the hat into clear wax as before to consolidate and smooth it. Use a wicking needle to pierce a hole just below the point of the hat. Thread the wick of the candle through the hole and pull the hat down on the wizard's head.

▶ The completed wizard is almost too good to burn, and would make a wonderful gift. Elaborate sculpted figure candles such as this are often kept as ornaments. Clean them of any dust under cold running water.

SCULPTING FLOWERS

Flower candles are always popular. These sculpted water lilies, formed from thin wax petals, can be used as floating candles and displayed in a variety of ways. They look particularly attractive when floated with real leaves in a shallow bowl as a table centerpiece.

YOU WILL NEED
6 oz. dip and carve wax—
  2 oz. dyed yellow,
  4 oz. dyed pale blue
Smooth board or work
  surface
Vegetable oil
Small pouring jug
Craft knife
Primed 1 in. wick, 2 in.
  long
Wax glue, melted in a
  small pot, and a small
  brush
Hair drier

1 Oil the board very sparingly so that the poured wax will not stick. Heat some yellow dip and carve wax until it has melted, and pour the wax on the board to make a thin sheet. When the wax has cooled to a pliable state, use a craft knife to cut out a long, low triangle to form into the flower center. Pull away the rest of the wax sheet and free the triangle from the board.

2 Lay the primed wick along the short edge of the triangle, and roll it up tightly towards the point. As you roll, keep the bottom edge aligned straight. This will be the base of the candle.

3 Press the completed flower center down on the board while it is still soft to flatten the base. This center needs to be compact around the wick for the candle to burn well.

4 Pour out a sheet of pale blue wax. When the wax has cooled sufficiently, cut out two petals, pointed at their tips. Pinch all round the edge of one petal, and wrap it around the outside of the yellow center. Use melted wax glue to make it adhere if necessary. Repeat for the second petal, positioning it opposite the first petal.

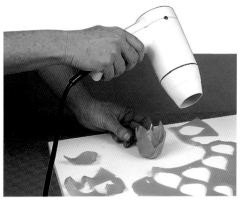

5 | Make several more petals and apply them to the outside of the flower. Shape each petal in your hands before applying, cupping them by pressing the center into your palm with your thumb. After applying, curve the petals inwards to partly conceal the flower center. You may have to pour further sheets of wax as you work if the wax cools too much to form properly.

7 | You can use a hair drier to extend the working time of a poured sheet of wax. Use the hottest setting and pass the hot air stream over the wax surface, keeping it moving until the wax becomes softened and malleable.

VARIATION
The roses in the photograph were sculpted in a similar way to the water lilies, using poured sheets of either red or white wax. The wick was wrapped in the same way, using the main color, and rounded rose petals were built up on the central cone. The red rose has green wax leaves applied.

▼ The finished candle will stand on a flat surface if you do not wish to use it as a water candle, but be sure to place it on non-flammable material. Flatten the base on a piece of heated foil if necessary.

6 | Periodically, press the flower down into your cupped palm to gather the petals upwards, as they have a tendency to sag outwards. The candle needs to be reasonably compact in order to burn well.

8 | When you have built up several layers of petals, trim the wick to 1/2 in. Leave the candle to cool thoroughly. You can dip the base in hot clear wax to consolidate it. It is also a good idea to place the candle in a small bowl while it cools to prevent the petals from opening out and sagging.

Twisting

The simple process of twisting flattened tapers into spirals is an age-old technique that is sometimes mimicked with molds. These instructions show you how to twist candles the traditional way for an elegant result.

Because the candles have to be partially rolled flat and then twisted, they need to be warm and pliable. It is easiest to use freshly dipped tapers; or you can warm existing tapers by overdipping them about ten or more times to heat them. Alternatively, use one of the methods given for heating candles in plaiting.

There are several ways you can vary this basic technique. Overdipped, graded candles look very attractive, especially when grouped together. You can vary the twist so that there is only one complete twist in the center, or, if the candle is pliable enough, you can make several twists all the way up. Try just twisting the bottom half of the candle so that the top is kept straight. To twist matching candles that are identical, twist the first candle and then keep it lying beside you as you work on the next candle. Keep measuring the second against the first to match the twists.

☞
Plaiting, page 50
Overdipping, page 29

YOU WILL NEED
Warm taper
Rolling pin
Smooth surface to work on (wood, waxed paper, or baking parchment)

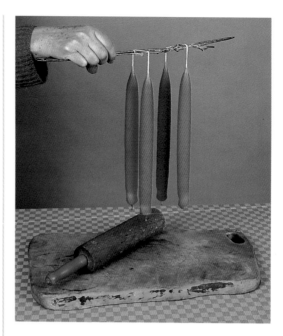

1 Before you begin, gather together all the materials. It is important to work fast while the candle is warm and pliable so be sure that you have everything you need before starting work.

2 Lay one of the tapers on the smooth board and roll it flat swiftly and firmly with the rolling pin. You will need to press quite hard to make it about 3/8 in. thick all along its length. Be careful that the rolling does not distort the surface of the candle; if you notice this beginning to happen, wait until the candle has cooled slightly.

3 Leave the top 1 in. unrolled and about the same at the base. Work up and down the length of the candle, rolling smoothly, to make it an even thickness.

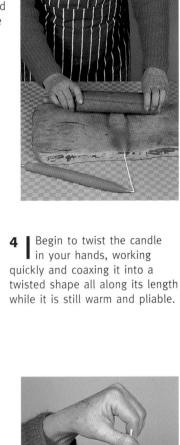

4 Begin to twist the candle in your hands, working quickly and coaxing it into a twisted shape all along its length while it is still warm and pliable.

5 Keep twisting and molding with your fingers to make an even twisted shape all the way up. Do not over-twist or the candle may begin to crack. Finally hold it up and turn it around to ensure that it is straight. You may need to shape the base a little if it has distorted so that it will fit neatly into a candleholder. Lay the candle aside to let it cool and set into its new shape.

▶ The finished candles burn well, despite their flattened centers. These candles look extremely attractive in a candelabra.

Water Candles

This is an exciting technique that produces fabulous swirls of paper-thin wax whirling around a candle like a magical cloak. As there is a large element of chance in making this type of candle, no two will ever be alike!

The formation of water candles makes use of the principle that wax floats on water. Molten wax is poured around a taper as it is lowered swiftly into a bucket of cold water. The wax attempts to float as it hardens and this causes the amazing formations typical of this type of candle. In this example, two consecutive layers of wax are applied, and the candle is twisted as it is plunged to make the beautiful swirls. The second application is in a different color that enhances the overall effect. Think carefully about the colors that you would like to use: white looks extremely beautiful and ethereal while pastels have great delicacy. You could also try using darker colors for a more mysterious look.

In this example, a simple taper is used for the base candle, but you could use a ball or pillar candle instead. Remember the candle needs to be easy to hold as you lower it into the water.

Water candles are very fragile so they have to be handled carefully. If you wish, you can add 1% hard microcrystalline wax to the melted wax to strengthen it.

YOU WILL NEED
Shallow bowl or dish, about 6 in. diameter	Heatproof jug
	Bucket of cold water
Vegetable oil	Small blue taper
13 oz. paraffin wax	Matches
Wax dyes—green and blue	
Knife or spatula	
Hard microcrystalline wax (optional)	

1 To make a wax disk, smear the inside of the dish with a thin coating of oil. This will make the disk easy to remove when it has set.

2 Melt about 5 oz. of wax with some green wax dye, and pour it into the dish. The disk needs to be at least ¹/₂ in. deep for strength. Leave until cool and completely set.

3 | Carefully ease the wax disk out of the dish with the knife. It should come away quite easily if you insert the tip of the knife under the edge.

4 | Use the knife to blunt and neaten the edge of the disk all round. You will find that the wax can be carved to shape easily.

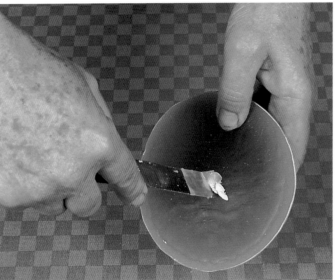

5 | Gouge a hole in the center of the disk with the knife, large enough to take the base of the taper. It needs to be fairly deep so that the taper can be inserted firmly.

6 | Melt the base of the taper with a match until it is beginning to drip, and quickly insert it into the hole in the disk.

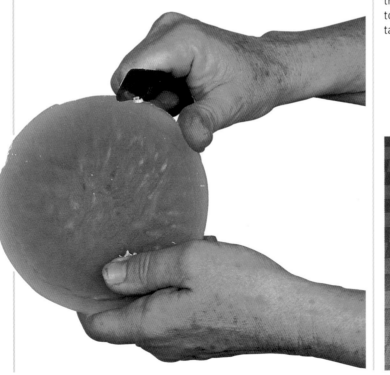

7 Hold the taper in the hole until the wax has set. This will be your handle for lowering the disk into the water, so you need to make it really strong.

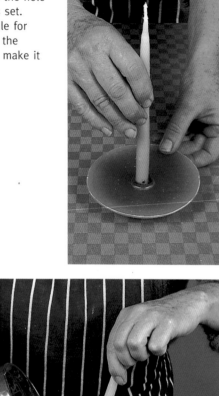

8 Melt about 4 oz. of wax with green wax dye. Add the microcrystalline wax at this point if you are using it. Heat to 165°F and pour it into the jug. Hold the taper and disk just above the water surface in the bucket and pour about ½ cup of wax on the disk. Immediately, plunge the disk into the bucket.

9 Still pouring wax in a thin stream, rotate the disk as the wax sets to give a swirled effect. Excess wax will set and float to the surface where it can be removed.

10 Carefully lift the candle from the bucket. The swirled effect from rotating the candle while pouring the wax is very marked.

TIP The temperature of the water in the bucket needs to be only as cold as ordinary tap water—about 50–60°F. At this temperature, the wax sets quickly but still gives you time to swirl it.

▼ When the water candle is lit, the thin swirls of wax glow quite magically. After the original taper has burnt down, you can replace it with another to make the candle everlasting, although some of the delicate swirls near the flame may not survive.

11 Repeat the process with the second wax color for more swirls. Melt the remaining wax with blue wax dye and pour it into the jug. Repeat as before, applying small splashes of wax on the disk and also higher up on the green swirls, pushing the candle downward into the water with each splash.

12 Finally you can break off any excess pieces of wax to refine the shape. Up-end the candle to pour off any water that is trapped inside.

EMBELLISHING TECHNIQUES

The art of embellishing candles adds a whole new dimension to candlemaking and is an opportunity to enjoy many other crafts as well. This section shows you how to create sumptuous candles for every occasion. You can embellish candles you have made yourself or use ready-made candles.

Appliqué with Flat Shapes

Appliqué is the technique of applying cutout wax shapes to candles. The leaves shown here are popular appliqué motifs, but you could use any simple shapes such as hearts, stars, stripes, or a combination of several different ones.

This sequence shows you how to pour your own sheets of wax and cut out shapes with small cutters. Cookie cutters are ideal, or you can use the smaller cutters available from cake decorating shops that are used for gum paste craft. The latter come in a wonderful variety of shapes, largely based on flowers and leaves, but including many other exotic shapes. Some, like the ivy leaf cutter shown here, have leaf veins built into the cutter that leave a stamped impression on the wax as you cut out the shape.

The best wax for this technique is dip and carve wax, or else paraffin wax with a low melting point. Otherwise the wax will cool too fast, and when you try to press the shapes on the curved candle, they may crack.

It is also possible to buy sheets of colored appliqué wax from candlemaking suppliers, some of which have different shapes already cut out. To use these, pull off the backing paper and press them on the candle.

YOU WILL NEED
Smooth board or work surface
Vegetable oil
3 oz. dip and carve wax, dyed green
Ivy leaf cutter
Sharp craft knife
White pillar candle
Wax glue, melted in a small pot
Brush
Gold paint and a fine paintbrush

1 Lightly oil the board. Melt the wax and pour out a small sheet of wax on the board. Allow the wax sheet to cool until the surface is set, but the wax is still soft and pliable. Use the ivy cutter to stamp out a few leaves.

2 You may find that a wax shape sometimes remains in the cutter after stamping. Use a craft knife to ease it out carefully.

3 This particular cutter has veins inside that impress on the surface of the wax. Alternatively, use a real leaf to impress lifelike veins on your wax leaves. Press the leaf on the cutout shapes, underside down, for the best impressions.

4 Work quickly so that the shapes remain pliable. Paint the back of each leaf with melted wax glue, and press it firmly on the candle.

5 Work up the candle, arranging the leaves in an attractive spray, and angling them outwards alternately. If you have several sizes of cutter, place larger leaves at the bottom of the candle, and smaller leaves at the top to simulate real ivy.

VARIATION
This candle is decorated in a similar appliqué technique, using large leaf cutters. The leaves were painted gold after being applied to the candle. The attractive base is made by standing the pillar candle in an oiled, shallow pan and pouring in a $1/2$ in. layer of white wax. Leave to set, then remove from the pan and carve off the edges to give an irregular effect.

▼ Various leaf shapes have been used to decorate these candles. However, there are many different cookie cutter designs available. Stars, moons, hearts and bells all suit this technique, or you can customize the decoration to suit specific festivals.

6 Paint a fine gold line between the leaves to suggest a curving stalk. Alternatively, cut and apply a very thin strip of wax.

Appliqué with Shaped Wax

Cutout pieces of wax can be modeled into three-dimensional shapes for appliqué to give charming results. Here, tiny pink flowers are shaped and applied to an egg-shaped candle.

Shaping wax after cutting it out is not difficult but you will need to work fairly quickly so that the wax remains malleable. Once it hardens, any pressure on it will cause it to crack. Keep a hair drier handy so that you can warm the wax if it cools too quickly. The techniques used here are very similar to gum paste flower-making in cake decorating.

The flowers are built up using a simple heart cutter for the petals and a star cutter for the flower centers. A ball tool is used to cup each petal before applying it, but you can use the back of a small teaspoon instead.

You can either use wax glue to attach the flower shapes to the candle or, alternatively, dip the back of each flower into hot, clear wax before applying it.

Dip and carve wax is the best kind to use, but you could use paraffin wax with a low melting point instead.

☞
Coloring, pages 16–17

YOU WILL NEED
Smooth board or work surface
Vegetable oil
3 oz. dip and carve wax—
    2 oz. dyed pink, 1 oz. dyed yellow
Small heart cutter
Small star cutter
Sharp craft knife
White egg candle
Ball tool
Wax glue, melted in a small pot
Brush
Hair drier

1 Lightly oil the board. Melt the pink wax and pour out a small sheet on the board. Allow the wax sheet to cool until the surface is set, but the wax is still soft and malleable.

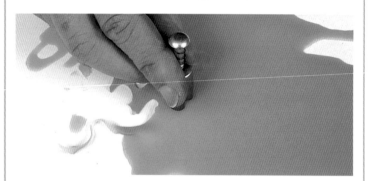

2 Use the heart cutter to stamp out the petals. This type of cutter has an integral plunger so that if the wax becomes stuck in the cutter, the little plunger will push it out.

3 Use a craft knife to lift the edges off the wax sheet and peel the waste wax away from around the petals. Carefully free each petal from the board by slicing under it with the knife.

4 Holding a petal on your finger, use the ball tool to press round the edge of the petal to thin it slightly. "Cup" it by pressing the ball tool into the center of the petal, which will curve it into a little cup-shape.

TIP Try making flowers in different color schemes and using different shaped candles. For example, white wax flowers trailing down a dark blue taper look very delicate and pretty.

5 Paint hot wax glue on the back of the pointed base of the petal and press it on the candle. Repeat with three or four more petals, placing their points together at the center of the flower. Repeat for two more flowers.

7 Apply wax glue to the back of each star and press it firmly into the center of a flower. Use the ball tool to indent the center of the star—this will raise the points of the star slightly to form a pretty flower center.

6 Pour out a small sheet of yellow wax on the board, and allow to cool until just set but still pliable. Use the star cutter to cut out small stars for the center of the flowers. Lift and remove the waste wax from around the stars, and carefully lift the stars from the board with the craft knife.

▶ The candle flame makes the semi-translucent flowers glow magically. However, remember that the flowers are fragile and easily damaged.

Découpage

Découpage, or the craft of applying cutout decorated paper to objects, adapts beautifully for embellishing candles. Here, a design is drawn on tissue paper, which is then applied to the candle.

When decorated tissue paper is attached to a candle and then dipped, the tissue becomes almost invisible and the design, here gold calligraphy, stands out. You can use this technique on any color of candle—just match the color with the same colored tissue paper. As an alternative to decorative writing with a gold pen, you can use rubber stamps to decorate the tissue paper. These can be obtained in an astonishing range of designs with inkpads of all colors, so you can use them to embellish candles for any event or occasion.

There is a wonderful choice of tissue paper available for this technique. It comes in a rainbow of colors for decorating yourself, and in many glorious printed designs as gift wrap or paper napkins. Any of these types of tissue paper can be used to embellish candles. Paper napkins in particular are available in designs for every holiday or festive situation so you can make your candles to match.

Do not leave candles embellished in this way unattended while burning. You may need to trim away the paper as the candle burns down.

YOU WILL NEED
Sheet of plain, or lined
  paper, and felt-tip pen
White pillar candle
White tissue paper
Scissors
Thick-nibbed gold
  permanent marker pen
Teaspoon
Tea light
Dipping can with clear
  paraffin wax for
  overdipping

☞
Transfers, page 111
Overdipping, page 31

1 First, plan your design by sketching it on rough paper. This design consists of hand-written lettering of the word "candle" in several languages sloping at an angle across the sheet, with simple stars between.

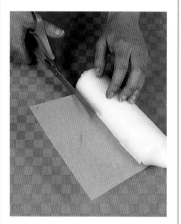

2 Lay the candle on the tracing paper, and cut out a piece to fit exactly round the sides of the candle. The two edges need to butt together where they meet.

3 Lay the tissue paper over your sketched design, and use the gold pen to trace the design. You may need to reposition the tissue paper several times to ensure that it is completely covered with the design right up to the edges.

4 Lay the decorated tissue paper over the candle and wrap it round tightly. If there are any gaps in the design, use the gold pen to draw small stars to fill them.

5 | Holding the tissue paper tightly round the candle, heat a teaspoon over a tea light flame, and press it on the tissue paper in the spaces between the gold lettering. The heat from the spoon will melt the wax below and stick the tissue paper to the candle. Do not hold the teaspoon right in the tea light flame, or it will become blackened with soot and could spoil the candle.

6 | Continue to work round the candle, pressing the tissue paper on with the back of the hot spoon. Make sure that the edges are well sealed. Avoid touching the gold lines with the spoon as they may smear.

7 | When the tissue is secured all round the candle, dip the candle once into clear paraffin wax. This will seal the tissue on the candle. When covered in wax, the tissue will become translucent and barely visible—the candle will appear to be decorated purely with gold writing. Leave the candle to cool and if necessary flatten the base.

VARIATION

An alternative to embellishing the candle with tissue that you have decorated yourself is to use one of the many attractive designs on paper napkins. Separate the decorated sheet from the others, and cut this to fit your candle. Continue as above for steps 5–7.

▼ Découpage candles have an air of professional elegance. As they burn down, the flame lights the tissue paper from within and makes each candle glow like a decorative lantern.

Dried Flowers

Moss and colorful dried flowers are used to

embellish candles in this attractive

technique. You can choose

flowers and candles to match

the color scheme of a room or

table setting.

Dried flowers combine well with candles, and they form a pleasing contrast to the glossy translucence of the wax. The flammability of dried plant material means that you should never leave these candles unattended when they are lit. Take care to decorate just the lower parts of the candle, and do not allow it to burn down as far as the decorations without removing them first.

It is possible to buy dried flowers, leaves, moss, and seed heads in a kaleidoscope of colors from craft shops and florists. If you have a garden, you can also grow and dry your own material, and there are many books available on this subject.

Plain candles look best with this technique and sturdy pillar candles are safest because they are less likely to topple on the dried plants. You can plan some wonderful color schemes, matching the candles to the flowers or choosing colors to contrast and enhance.

☞
**Pressed Flowers, pages
104–105
Wrapping, pages
114–115**

YOU WILL NEED
Yellow pillar candle
Dried moss
Dried flowers—small
    sprays and larger
    flower heads
Scissors
PVA glue

1 A yellow pillar candle has been chosen to complement the shades of orange of the dried flowers. Tease out the moss and arrange it round the base of the candle to judge how much you need before applying the glue. It should make a thick layer around the bottom 2–2$\frac{1}{2}$ in. of the candle.

2 Squeeze out the glue generously to cover the base of the candle in a zigzag line. This line of glue will hold the moss more effectively than a continuous coating.

3 Stand the candle upright on a work surface, and wrap the moss around the base, pressing it firmly on the glue. You need to cover the entire base of the candle with moss. This will give you a surface that is easier for gluing the flowers on than the smooth wax. Leave the glue to dry for a while.

4 Cut some sprays of smaller flowers to length, holding them against the candle to decide on your design. Sprays angling out from a center point at the base of the candle work well as you can cover the stalks with larger flower heads. Apply glue generously to one side of each spray and press it on the moss.

TIP You can dry your own moss in a microwave oven. Pick one or two handfuls of moss and remove any earth from the roots. Place it in an absorbent, brown paper bag and turn over the top. Set your microwave on half power and microwave in three-minute bursts, checking the moss after each. It usually takes about 10 minutes for the moss to dry and it should still retain its bright green color.

▼ The finished candles have a lovely natural effect, and give the appearance of emerging from miniature mossy gardens.

5 Apply more sprays, working around the candle and taking care not to dislodge the pieces you have already applied. The glue dries quite slowly, so you can reposition any sprays if you wish. Add a few seed heads, or taller sprays above the small sprays. Cut off the stalks of some larger flower heads and glue them to the base of the sprays, covering the stalks.

6 Hold the material on the candle firmly for a minute or two to be sure it is securely glued. At this point you can glue down any pieces that are not firm.

Dripping

Wax can be dripped on candles in a variety of ways to create some beautiful effects. In the techniques shown here, microcrystalline wax has been used for a frosty result.

Any shape of candle can be used for this technique, but different shapes will affect the way that the melted wax drips down the candle. The sequence here shows two ways of dripping: pouring wax centrally on the top of a candle, and pouring evenly spaced splashes on a candle held horizontally.

There are many other ways you can vary the effect; for example, coloured candles with dark, contrasting wax drippings can look very dramatic. Hard microcrystalline wax has a high melting point, so besides giving an attractive frosted result, it hardens quickly on the candle so that the drips are thicker than if you used ordinary paraffin wax.

YOU WILL NEED
8 oz. hard microcrystalline wax
Board or pan to catch excess wax
Small jug for each color
Board
Knife
For the ball candle:
White ball candle
Wax dye—yellow and terracotta
For the taper:
White taper
Wax dye—red and green
Gold paint and small brush

☞
Dripping (Making Techniques), pages 32–33

THE BALL CANDLE

1 Melt 2 oz. hard microcrystalline wax with yellow wax dye and transfer it to a small, heated jug. Place the ball candle on the board surface, or in a pan to catch the excess wax. Slowly drizzle the yellow wax over the top of the candle, allowing it to run down the sides in streams.

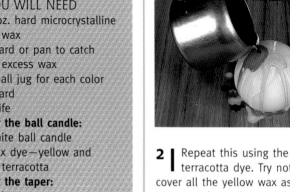

2 Repeat this using the terracotta dye. Try not to cover all the yellow wax as you pour, but enhance it by pouring streams between the yellow drips.

3 Leave the candle to cool. As the microcrystalline wax cools, a frosty texture will appear. The dripped wax on the board can be scraped off and used again.

4 Carefully remove the candle from the board. You may need to use your knife to cut round the base to free it. Now trim away the dripped wax around the base to neaten it.

THE TAPER

1 Melt 2 oz. hard microcrystalline wax with red wax dye, and pour it into a small, heated jug. Hold the taper horizontally over the board or pan, and pour a slow stream of the melted wax on the candle at regular intervals along its length. Allow the wax to flow down on both sides of the candle where it will form a drip under each pouring point. Hold the candle in this position until the wax has cooled.

2 Repeat this using green wax dye, and pour at regular intervals in the spaces between the red wax. Sections of the white candle should show between the colored wax splashes as here, or you can allow the layers of poured wax to overlap each other.

3 Leave the candle to cool. The poured wax will have left a row of drips on either side of the candle. Emphasize each drip with a dab of gold paint applied with a brush.

▶ The finished candles are extremely decorative. The orange taper is decorated in the same way as the red and green taper and shows how the separate pours of wax form strong, triangular shapes on the candle sides.

Embossing

Embossed candles are usually molded from flexible molds and there is a remarkable variety available. However, simple dipped or molded candles can be beautifully embossed in other ways, and three ideas are given here.

2 The glue will cool and harden rapidly, and as it melts the candle slightly where it lies, it will be stuck firmly to the candle surface. You can turn the candle slowly as you work, but be sure the glue has cooled before you touch it—although low melt glue-guns operate at a low temperature so you are unlikely to burn yourself.

GLUE-GUN EMBOSSING

A glue-gun can be used to emboss candles with random, curling lines. This gives remarkably high relief that can be further embellished with gold paint. As the glue used in glue-guns is non-flammable and non-toxic, it does not interfere with the burning of the candle; the glue just melts away as the candle burns.

YOU WILL NEED
Glue-gun and white glue
  sticks
Blue egg candle
For the white candle:
White taper
Gold paint (optional)

3 Finish the candle off by going over any places that have gaps. When you have finished, stop squeezing the trigger, and pull the gun away from the candle. You may find that fine threads of glue will string out from the candle, but these can be trimmed away with scissors when cool. Stand the candle upright to set.

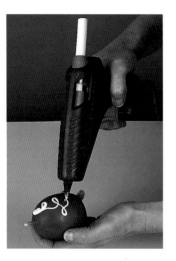

1 Heat the glue-gun until it is hot. Hold the candle over a surface protected with paper. Squeeze the trigger on the glue-gun until the glue begins to emerge, holding it about 1 in. above the candle surface. Allow the line of glue to fall on the candle, moving the glue-gun gently over the surface in circular motions. The glue will form a continuous line of curls and loops.

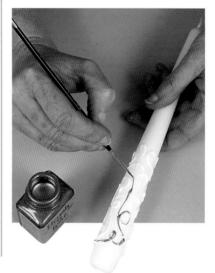

4 This taper candle has been embossed with the glue-gun over its lower half only. When the glue is completely cool, use a fine paintbrush and gold paint to highlight the embossed lines. This looks most effective when a candle has been embossed with glue of the same color as the wax.

RELIEF OUTLINER

A glass-painting relief outliner can be used to emboss candles. These are normally available in black, gold, and silver. The relief is not as high as with the glue-gun, but the tube and nozzle gives you better control so that intricate patterns can be achieved.

YOU WILL NEED
Glass paint relief outliner
Dark green ball candle

3 When the first motif is completed, draw others at evenly spaced intervals around the candle. Leave the candle to dry overnight. The relief outliner will flatten slightly as it dries.

▼ Shown below are the glue-gun embossed and the relief-outliner embossed candles. The light from the candle flame catches the embossing and enhances the elaborate designs.

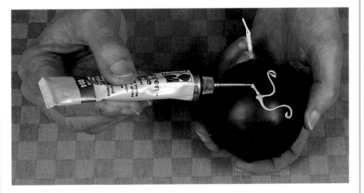

1 Hold the candle steadily in your palm and squeeze the tube of outliner gently to start the flow. It is best to practice a few strokes on paper first to judge the flow from the tube. Some tubes need constant pressure while others flow more freely. Make a small dot in the center of your design, and draw four curling lines out from this point.

2 Add further curls to the original lines. You will find it easier to draw an even line if you pull the tube rather than push it. To do this you will need to keep turning the candle round.

TJANTING

This technique uses a *tjanting*, a wax-painting tool that is normally used in Batik. The *tjanting*'s cup is filled with hot beeswax, and a steady drip will emerge from the nozzle that can be applied to candles to form simple dots and swirls. The resulting designs are delicate and unusual, and you can use a contrasting wax color, or the same colour as the candle for a more subtle effect. The relief design is fairly high and you can create very colorful embossed candles with several colors. Beeswax is the best wax to use for this technique as it is sticky and adheres well to the candle.

Practice using the *tjanting* on a piece of foil, or an old candle before you start, as the constant flow takes a little getting used to.

YOU WILL NEED
Tjanting
2 oz. beeswax
Red wax dye
Small container for heating the wax
Kitchen paper towel or a rag
White taper

1 Melt the beeswax with the dye in a small pot or jug. Place the *tjanting* bowl into the wax for a few moments to heat it to the same temperature. Half fill the bowl with wax and hold it above the pot until it cools a little so that the flow reduces to a steady drip.

2 With paper towel handy to catch any drips, apply a line of small dots to the candle with the nozzle of the *tjanting*. The wax temperature affects the rate of flow—it is much faster when the wax is hot, so you can adjust the flow by allowing the wax in the *tjanting* bowl to cool, or by reheating it in the wax pot.

3 When the wax stops flowing, place the *tjanting* back in the pot to heat and refill it. Finish off the end of each line of dots with an "S" scroll by moving the *tjanting* over the surface as the wax flows.

4 Repeat the line of dots around the candle at different lengths. Stand the candle upright in a candleholder to cool. The embossed wax will be in high relief, but will be easily damaged so treat these candles with care. Clean the *tjanting* with hot water to melt away any remaining wax.

▼ The finished candle shows the high relief achievable with the *tjanting*. You could try to use this embossing technique on ball and pillar candles, where the greater surface area gives scope for more elaborate designs.

Foils

These candles have been decorated with ordinary aluminum foil that has been folded and cut into simple motifs using the ancient craft of paper cutting. For a colored result you could use glass paints on the foil after attaching it to the candle.

Aluminum foil is particularly successful for this technique, as it is robust and can be burnished to a smooth finish. You can use either the matte or the shiny side depending on the effect you want to achieve. The silver of the aluminum combines well with the white candle, but the effect looks equally attractive on colored candles. As an alternative, try using the colored foils from sweet wrappings or the foils available for gift wrap. You have to make sure that they are true foils, and not plastic which can give off harmful fumes if burnt.

This technique works best with a pillar or taper candle because the foil will not curve round the sides of a ball or other rounded candle.

A swan motif is provided here for you to trace, but you could use any other motif of approximately the same size. A ring of little figures holding hands is a traditional motif for paper folding and cutting and there are many other ideas you could try such as fish, flowers, and trees. The technique is very quick to do, as you only have to cut out the motif once to get a repeat that goes all round the candle.

YOU WILL NEED
White pillar candle
Aluminum foil
Tracing paper and pencil
Sharp scissors
Teaspoon
Tea light or small candle
Sequins
Wax glue

☞
Gold leaf, pages 90–91

1 Cut a strip of foil that is about half as high as the candle. Wrap it around the candle base and mark where the ends should meet for an exact fit.

2 Cut the foil straight across at the mark. Try to avoid crumpling the foil as much as possible. You will be able to burnish it smooth at a later point, but creases are best avoided if possible, as they are hard to remove completely.

3 Fold the foil strip in half, then fold it again and a third time. How many folds are needed depends on the thickness of the candle and so the length of the strip. You will need the final area to be about 2 in. wide so there is sufficient space to draw a motif. Open out the foil and the folds will show as marks where you need to re-fold.

4 Fold the foil up again, along the same fold lines, but this time in a concertina shape. You can open it out to check that it looks as shown here, then fold it back tightly.

6 Cut out the motif through all the layers of the folded foil, but remember that the beak and tail feathers will form the link between the foil sections so do not cut through them.

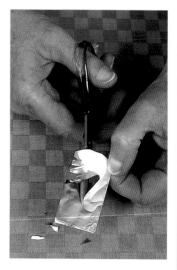

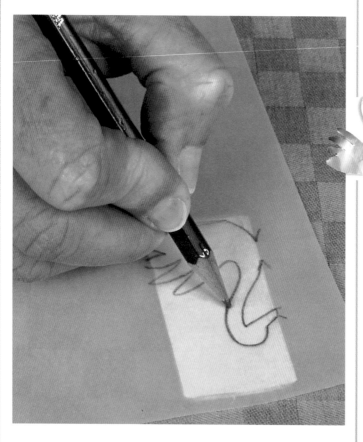

7 Carefully open out the foil sections, avoiding any tears. You may need to slip the point of the scissors between the sections to open them out if they are folded together very tightly.

5 Trace the swan motif, adjusting it if necessary so that it will fit on one section of the foil. The beak and the tail feathers should just reach the edges on either side. Lay the tracing paper on the top of the folded foil and draw over the design, pressing lightly to mark the design on the foil.

8 Lay the foil on a smooth surface and burnish the folds with the back of a teaspoon to smooth them as much as possible. If you wish to give a texture to the foil, burnish it on top of a piece of fabric.

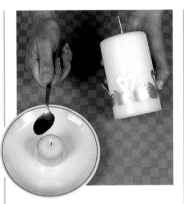

9 | Wrap the foil tightly around the candle, holding it in place with a dab of wax glue. Heat the back of a teaspoon over the flame of a tea light or a small candle. Do not hold the spoon right in the flame or it will be blackened by soot.

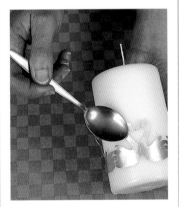

10 | Press the hot teaspoon against the foil to melt the wax beneath and so stick it down firmly. Try to avoid touching the bare wax surface with the spoon because you will make visible marks.

11 | Use the handle of the teaspoon or a brush to apply wax glue to the back of sequins and dot them around the candle surface above the swans. Snowflake sequins have been used here for an attractive picture effect.

▶ The smooth foil shapes on the white candle have a pleasing simplicity. Simple patterns are the easiest to unfold and apply to a candle. If you cut out a more intricate pattern, you will need to take care that you do not tear the foil when unfolding it.

TEMPLATE
Enlarge or reduce the swan template on a photocopier to fit the folded foil.

Gold Leaf

Candles embellished with gold leaf are the ultimate luxury as the candlelight flickers and highlights the gold. These candles have been decorated with artificial leaf, or "Dutch leaf," which is much cheaper than true gold leaf, and looks just as effective.

True gold leaf is a very thin, beaten layer of pure gold that is applied to various surfaces using a coat of size as adhesive. Artificial, or "Dutch leaf," is very similar in appearance but only a fraction of the cost and comes in gold, silver, and copper colors as well as several multi-colored designs.

As size will not stick successfully to candle wax, the best way to apply the leafs is to lay them on the candle surface and apply heat to melt the wax underneath. This will stick the leafs to the candle surface. The torn edges of the gold leaf gives a lovely random effect to the candles and you can further add to the abstract effect by scuffing away some of the leaf or even mixing different colored leafs in layers.

Artificial leaf should always be varnished after applying otherwise it will dull and tarnish in time. Use an ordinary hobby varnish or one of the special candle varnishes sold by candlemaking suppliers. You are only applying one layer of varnish, so it will not give off fumes. However, use candle varnish if you are concerned.

☞
Foils, pages 87–89

YOU WILL NEED
Artificial gold leaf
White taper
Soft paintbrush
Teaspoon
Bowl of boiling water
Rag or paper kitchen towel
Varnish and brush

1 First assemble your materials. The artificial leaf usually comes in loose sheets, each placed between sheets of tissue paper. Remember that it is very fragile and the slightest draft will blow it away!

2 Wash and dry your hands thoroughly because any grease will tarnish the gold leaf. Pick up the edge of a sheet of leaf and tear off a strip by pulling it apart gently.

3 Lay the strip on the bottom of the taper, angling it across the candle. You can lift it off the candle and reposition it if you wish.

4 Brush all over the applied leaf with a soft paintbrush to smooth it on the candle surface. Brushing should eliminate any wrinkles or air bubbles under the leaf, but do not worry if there is a little irregularity as this can add to the effect of texture in the gold.

7 When you have finished applying the leaf, paint the leaf-covered part of the candle with varnish to prevent the artificial leaf tarnishing. When using real gold leaf, there is no need to varnish.

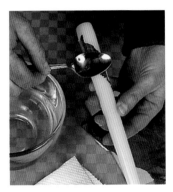

5 To fix the gold leaf more firmly on the candle, dip a teaspoon into some freshly boiled water to heat it, mop it dry, and press it on the leaf, burnishing it up and down. The heat from the spoon will melt the wax underneath the leaf and stick it down. Alternatively you can heat the teaspoon over a tea-light flame.

6 Tear off another strip of leaf and apply it to the candle in the same way. Long thin strips of leaf, applied at the same angle with gaps between them look very attractive, or you can cover the bottom of the candle with a continuous layer of leaf.

▶ The gold leaf on white casts shadows into the wax beneath to give a dark background to the gold. The burgandy candle shows how effective this technique is on a dark candle. The leaf will not affect the burning properties of the candles.

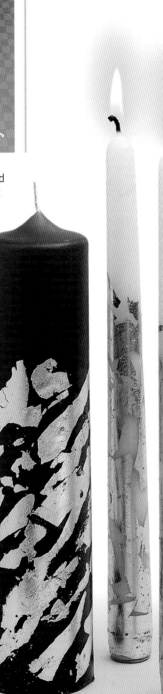

Incising

The soft surface of wax can be incised to produce some lovely effects, especially if the candle has been overdipped so that the cuts reveal a different colored wax beneath. When these ball candles burn down a little, the flame glows through the candle and lights up the incised design.

A lino-cutting tool with a "V"-shaped blade is the ideal tool for incising candles. It leaves a clean cut that reaches down into the white wax of the candle. Use the lino-cutter by pushing it at a shallow angle into the wax so that it cuts a shallow groove. The initial cut need not be deep as you can go over each cut again to deepen it. If you do not have a lino-cutting tool, use a sharp knife instead. Alternative tools for this technique include a pyrography iron, a heated nail, or a metal skewer. These will melt grooves in the wax rather than incise it, but still give a lovely result.

Dip and carve wax is used for overdipping a basic white candle as it is far less likely to shatter when being incised. An alternative is to use paraffin wax with a low melting point.

Choose simple motifs for this technique—straight lines are far easier to cut than curved lines. For variety, try dipping a candle in two different colors before incising. A dark-colored candle overdipped in chalky white wax looks very dramatic, with the incised lines showing dark against a light background.

YOU WILL NEED
White ball candle
4 oz. dip and carve wax
Blue wax dye
Dipping can
Pencil
Lino-cutting tool
Large soft paintbrush

☞
**Overdipping,
page 31**

1 Heat the wax with the wax dye, and pour a layer on the surface of hot water in the dipping can. Hold the candle by its wick and dip it into the wax.

2 Allow the candle to cool for at least 30 seconds, then dip again, repeating until a layer of blue wax, about 1/8 in. thick, has built up on the candle surface. Any drips underneath the candle can be trimmed off afterwards.

3 Use a pencil to lightly sketch your design on the wax surface. To make a snowflake, draw a simple six-sided star as a guide. Start with a line and then draw a cross through the center, keeping the arms at equal intervals apart.

4 Use the lino-cutting tool to incise the design. First cut the arms of the snowflake by pushing the tool through the wax to make shallow grooves. After the initial line cut, you can deepen the groove further. Do not try to cut too deep the first time or the tool will bury itself in the wax and shatter the blue coating. Brush loose wax away with the soft paintbrush.

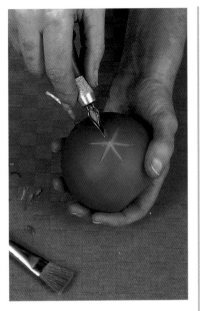

7 When the large snowflakes are completed, cut small stars in between to fill the spaces. Although smaller, they should be cut to the same depth as the larger motifs.

▼ Incised candles have a pleasing combination of texture and color. The green candle has been incised with simple feather motifs using the same technique.

5 Embellish the arms of the snowflake with shorter cuts. You can also fill the spaces between the arms with smaller lines and arrows.

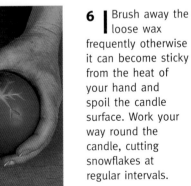

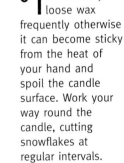

6 Brush away the loose wax frequently otherwise it can become sticky from the heat of your hand and spoil the candle surface. Work your way round the candle, cutting snowflakes at regular intervals.

Inclusions

Candles with inclusions have an ethereal quality that is quite enchanting. Silk or dried flowers, herbs, or even shells and pebbles are set into translucent wax around a core candle so that they are just visible in a delicate veil of wax.

You can use any material you like for candle inclusions provided that it is dry, and will not react with the wax, or be dangerous when burnt. Pebbles, shells, glass beads or nuggets, marbles, broken china pieces, and metal charms are all successful inclusions. As they are heavier than wax, they will sink to the bottom of the mold, which is usually the top of the candle. You will have to bear this in mind when adding the inclusions if you do not have enough to reach the top of the mold.

Silk and paper flowers, pot pourri, and dried flowers, leaves, herbs, and fruit can be used successfully as well, despite their potentially flammable nature. Use a fairly wide core candle so that when the candle burns down, the material is well away from the flame. These candles are particularly beautiful so they are well worth making although they should never be left unattended when burnt.

It is important to use wax that is as translucent as possible for candles with inclusions so do not add any Stearin. You will therefore need to oil the mold or use mold release.

☞
**Molding,
pages 38–49**

YOU WILL NEED
Rigid candle mold
Vegetable oil and brush
White taper
Sharp knife
Cutting board
Mold seal
Dried heather sprays
Paraffin wax (sufficient
    amount for the mold)
Water bath (optional)

SAFETY
When burning a candle that contains inclusions, you should allow for the fact that the added material may affect the burning quality of the candle. The thicker the core candle, the less of a problem this will be as the core candle will burn down in a cavity in the center of the candle and the inclusions will be away from the flame. With most inclusion candles, it is advisable, once the candle has burned down a short distance, to insert a tea light into the resulting depression and replace this as necessary.

1 Lightly brush over the inside of the mold with vegetable oil. Wipe away any excess oil, which would otherwise spoil the surface of the finished candle.

2 Insert the taper wick end downward in your chosen mold, and mark off where it reaches the top of the mold. Lay the candle on a cutting board and cut the base off so that the candle is about 1/2 in. shorter than this measurement.

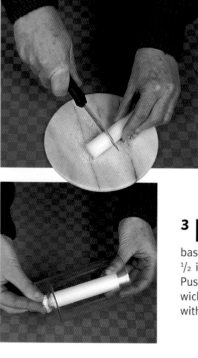

3 Insert the candle wick down into the mold. The base should now be about 1/2 in. shorter than the mold. Push the wick through the wick hole and seal it firmly with mold seal.

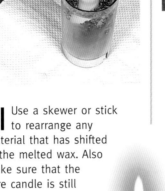

7 When the candle is completely cool, remove the mold seal and slide the candle out of the mold. The inclusions should be clearly visible through the sides of the candle.

▼ When these candles are lit, they become pillars of light, with the lovely natural forms of the inclusions visible in the wax. The completed heather candle is shown here with two variations: one contains dried orange slices, the other blue silk flowers.

4 Arrange your inclusions in the space between the core candle and the sides of the mold. The inclusions closest to the outer walls will be the most visible, so pay particular attention to those. Dried plant material might float when the wax is poured so try to jam it firmly into the space.

6 Use a skewer or stick to rearrange any material that has shifted in the melted wax. Also make sure that the core candle is still central in the mold. Place the mold in a water bath, if you are using one, and cool down and top up the candle just like a basic molded candle.

5 Heat the wax to 185–190°F. A fairly hot temperature is needed because the inclusions will quickly cool the wax. Use a small, heated jug to pour the wax into the space between the mold and the core candle.

Marbling

There are several ways of embellishing candles to produce marbled colors and these instructions describe two contrasting techniques: the first shows how to marble using concentrated dyes and a blow torch, the second uses a technique of denting, dipping, and peeling to give unpredictable effects of color.

Marbling can be used in combination with other techniques such as wax painting or gold leaf, but be sure to marble the candle first before applying other embellishments as the blow torch could destroy the other designs.

Choose the colors for marbling carefully. Here we use the three primary colors, which combine beautifully with each other to create rainbow effects, but just two or even one color can be equally effective. The color of the candle used will also affect the result and very dark candles can look stunning with strong applications of dye.

YOU WILL NEED
White candle
Wax dyes (powder or wax disks) in several colors
Knife
Blow torch

☞
Gold leaf, pages 90–91
Scenting, pages 18–19

MARBLING WITH A BLOW TORCH

This technique is sometimes called "tie-dye" as it mimics the effects of that technique in fabric dyeing. It can be used on candles of all sizes and shapes. Here it is demonstrated on a taper and a ball candle, but it can be equally effective on large pillar candles, the top surface of sand candles, and on container candles.

1 | Holding the candle as flat as possible, use the knife tip to scoop up small quantities of powder dye and tip them on the candle surface. If you are using dye disks, shave off a few shreds to lay on the candle. You can also melt the shreds in a small spoon over a tea light and drizzle on the candle.

2 | Powder dyes are very concentrated so only use tiny quantities, as shown. They are also liable to slip off the candle, so you will need to keep it level.

3 | Using the blow torch on a low heat, lightly pass the flame over the powders. The candle surface will begin to melt and the powders will quickly combine with the molten wax, running into attractive swirls of color.

4 The colors will begin to merge together and form new colors. Do not overheat or the wax will drip. The force of the flame will cause the colors to move away from it and this can be used to advantage to push the colors where you want them to go.

6 This technique looks very effective with ball candles as the dye can be applied to the top surface and then torched down the sides. For added safety, place the candle on a flameproof surface such as a metal baking sheet before torching.

▼ The finished candles have lovely swirls of molten color across their surfaces. For a darker result, you can torch several layers of color onto the candles

5 Continue working the colors around the candle. To color the other side of the candle, allow it to cool briefly and then repeat the process on the other side, adding more powder color and torching it around the candle.

7 The finished ball candle shows how the powder colors have combined with the melted wax and flowed down the candle in streaks that aptly mimic flames.

MARBLING WITH A HAMMER

This technique produces a speckled type of marbling, and the results are very variable depending on the color of the overdipping wax and the shape of the hammer or tool used to dent the candle. Dipping the candle serves not only to change the color of the candle, but also softens it so that the hammer blows dent it more easily.

Dip and carve wax is used here so that the colored coatings are less likely to crack when hammered or carved. You can use paraffin wax with a low melting point instead.

YOU WILL NEED
White ball candle
Old towel
Hammer
4 oz. dip and carve wax
Wax dye—yellow and red
Dipping can
Sharp knife

☞
Overdipping, page 31

1 Place the towel on a firm surface and lay the candle on it. The towel will pad the back of the candle and prevent it from being crushed. Hammer the candle all over with quite hard blows—you want to distort the surface of the candle, but not crush it.

2 Melt the dip and carve wax and add the yellow wax dye. Fill the dipping can with boiling water and add the melted wax. Dip the candle several times to build up about a ⅛ in. layer of yellow wax.

3 Allow the candle to cool for one or two minutes, and hammer it again, making dents all over the soft surface.

The white base color of the candle will be exposed as you hammer the yellow top coat.

4 Add some red dye, melted in a little wax, to the yellow wax dipping can. This will combine with the yellow to make a strong orange-red. Dip the candle into the mixture several times to build up to a similar thickness as the yellow layer.

5 | Allow the candle to cool for a few minutes. Using a sharp knife, pare away the top layer of the wax to reveal the colors underneath. The red wax will have filled the deeper depressions and will remain visible, while the yellow and white layers are exposed in a random pattern. You can give the candle a final dip in hot, clear wax to finish it off or leave it undipped if you want the colors to be sharper.

▶ The hammered blue and red ball candle at the front has been given a final dip in clear wax; the red and yellow candle has been left undipped. The swirled effect on the other three candles was achieved with glass paint marbling (see above).

VARIATION
The three swirled candles on the right have been marbled in yet another way, using glass paints. You will need alcohol-based glass paints, and a bowl of cold water. Drip several colors of glass paint on the surface of the water. Stir the floating drops gently with a skewer to swirl the colors and dip the candle into the water. The glass paint will cling to the candle surface in lovely marbled effects. Leave to dry overnight.

Painting

Painting candles is a very rewarding form
of embellishment because the smooth
sides of a candle are a perfect surface
for painting. Two materials are used
here: acrylic paints and wax.

PAINTING WITH ACRYLICS

Acrylic paints are water-based, permanent, and come in a large variety of colors. It is often suggested that they should be mixed with liquid detergent to make them adhere to the candle surface, but there is no need for this if a thin film of paint is applied to the candle first.

The best paints to use are artist's acrylics, which are available from art and craft shops. These have the highest quality pigments and are saturated colors that go on thickly. You can also use craft and hobby paints, which are less expensive although the covering will not be as good. Use quality artist's brushes with man-made fiber hairs because this type of paint can ruin sable brushes. You will find painting far easier if you use a good brush—cheap hobby brushes will never give you the same result.

When painting candles with acrylics, avoid covering the candle completely as this can affect the burning. Use the wax color of the candle as the background and paint on motifs and designs so that only a small percentage of the candle is covered with paint.

Folk art designs look particularly effective on candles and the rose design shown here is simple to achieve. However, there is no limit to what you can use as your inspiration!

☞
Stenciling, pages
108–110

YOU WILL NEED
Dark green ball candle
Acrylic paints—black,
    green, crimson, white,
    yellow
Soft rag
Paintbrush
Saucer for mixing
Water pot

1 Mix together green and black paint without adding water to make a dark green to match the color of the candle. Paint the mixture over the side of the candle you want to decorate, choosing a side that is smooth and free from blemishes.

2 Smear the paint across the candle with the rag, wiping away the excess but leaving a thin coating which will make the candle surface slightly matt. Allow to dry.

3 Mix the crimson paint with some white to make a medium pink. Use this to paint the center of the rose as two opposing curves. Paint the outer petals, leaving a slight gap between for the dark background to show through. Use only enough water to make the paint workable because you need it to be thick and opaque.

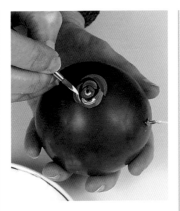

4 | Paint white highlights on the petals—a thin line along the side of each petal that would be exposed to the light. You can add to the sense of depth by mixing a darker pink and painting thin lines along the shadowed side of the petals, but avoid overworking—simplicity is more effective.

5 | Mix yellow and white paint with green to make a pale green for the leaves. Paint simple leaf shapes outside the rose, not quite touching the petals. Add streaks of yellow or darker green for a natural effect. Paint a dark green line in the center of each leaf.

6 | Finally paint sprays of small white flowers coming out from behind the rose. You can make the design symmetrical if you wish, but irregularity will give a more pleasing effect and is easier to achieve! Leave the paint to dry for several hours.

TIP | Alcohol-based glass paints can be used very sucessfully on candles, and you can paint them directly on the wax surface. They give beautiful stained glass effects when combined with relief outliner.

▼ The photograph shows a variety of motifs painted onto candles of different colors. The orange candle is scented with lemon oil as well as being painted with lemons.

PAINTING WITH WAX

Wax is the best medium for painting on candles because it will not affect the burning properties. However, it is not as easy to use as acrylic paint—as the wax cools quickly when loaded on the brush, it is difficult to complete each brush stroke before the wax has hardened. The way to overcome this problem is to use small glass jars set in a pan of boiling water for the colored wax. You may need to place the pan on a heat source to keep the water at simmering point to keep the wax hot enough.

Beeswax is the best wax to use for painting since it is sticky and will adhere well to the candle surface. It is also unlikely to flake off when cool. Use an old, fairly large brush, because the wax is virtually impossible to remove afterwards and the brush will have to be dedicated to wax painting.

The design used here of simple irises and leaves is inspired by Chinese brush painting. The rapid cooling of the wax gives little time for detail so bold brush strokes with a large brush are easiest to achieve.

YOU WILL NEED
White pillar candle
2 oz. beeswax
Wax dyes—dark green, violet, deep yellow
Three small glass jars or similar containers
Paintbrush
Pan of boiling water
Lino-cutting tool or knife

☞
Embossing, pages 84–86
Overdipping, page 31

1 | Place about ¹/₂ oz. of beeswax in each jar and put the jars in a pan of boiling water over a heat source until the wax has melted. The water should come halfway up the sides of the jars. Add wax dye to each jar to produce a strong color. Put the paintbrush into the green wax jar to heat it up.

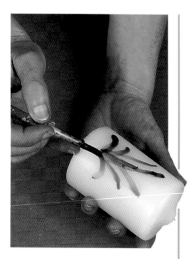

2 | Hold the candle firmly in your hand and load the brush with hot green wax. Brush the wax on in one continuous stroke to paint a leaf. You have to place the brush back in the hot wax for at least 30 seconds between each stroke to reheat and load again with hot wax. Paint several leaves and stems fanning out from a point at the base of the candle.

3 | Clean your brush by dipping it into hot water to melt away the wax. Next, soak your brush in the violet wax until it is warmed through. Load the brush with violet wax for the iris petals.

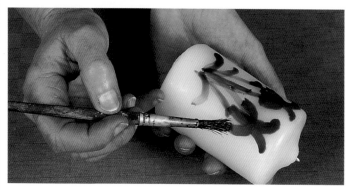

4 | Two upright petals and three lower petals are all that is needed for each flower, each petal requiring just one stroke. You can repeat a stroke if you wish to darken it, but avoid making too many different strokes or the result will be messy.

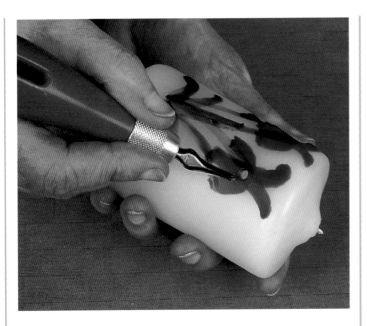

TIP Try combining wax painting with overdipping for landscape effects. Overdip the base of a candle in light green, then paint on details of grasses, trees, and flowers.

▼ The candle with the windmill design, inspired by Delft tiles, has been painted in the same way but using a finer brush. The colors used were blue, black, and orange.

5 Use the lino-cutting tool or a knife to carve out a small circle of the violet wax in the center of each iris to reveal the white wax below. You can use the same tool to cut away any mistakes or to thin the strokes. Clean your brush as before and paint a spot of the deep yellow wax in the center of each iris.

6 Finally add a few more leaves to balance the design. You can now paint the other side of the candle if you wish. The wax in the jars can be left to cool until solid and then kept until you next want to use them. In this way you can build up a palette of different wax colors for painting candles.

Pressed Flowers

The delicate effect of pressed flowers on candles is an old favorite that remains eternally popular. The technique is surprisingly simple to achieve and the delightful result evokes memories of summer meadows during long winter evenings.

White or cream candles are traditionally used for this technique as they complement the subtle colors of the flowers and leaves. You can use a flower press to press your flowers or simply use a thick book. Smaller flowers and feathery or fern-like leaves look particularly attractive on candles. Gather the plants on a dry day and lay them out, well spaced, on blotting paper. Cover with another sheet of blotting paper and press for several weeks until completely dry. Avoid flower heads that are very thick and fleshy for they will not press well and will be too bulky for applying to candles. A way to overcome this problem is to cut the flower head in half and press it with the cut side down; another method is to press the petals separately and then reassemble the whole flower on the candle. Do not forget to press plenty of leaves and stalks as well as flower heads.

YOU WILL NEED
White or cream candles
Pressed flowers
Glue pen with a sponge-
    tip applicator
Dipping can with clear
    paraffin wax

1 | Gather together the materials and arrange the pressed flowers on paper so that you can plan color schemes and arrangements. Pressed flowers look attractive on most shapes of candles.

2 | Arrange the plant material on the candle so as to plan the design. Narrow tapers will need smaller sprays than thicker candles. It is better to arrange the flowers and leaves in groups and sprays rather than simply dotting them over the candle surface.

3 | Apply glue to the back of a pressed leaf. You have to cover it with enough to hold the full length of the piece down on the candle.

4 | Press the leaf lightly on the candle. Repeat until you have completed your design. Be careful that you do not damage flowers that you have already stuck down when you work round the candle. While the glue is wet, you can carefully reposition pieces.

5 | Dip the candle once into the wax. The best temperature for the wax is about 180°F to make a really thin and transparent coating. You can dip one taper before decorating the other, but keep the tapers joined so that they can be hung for display after decorating.

6 | After dipping, press down any flowers or leaves that are sticking up through the wax and they should stay down, as the soft wax will hold them. As the wax cools, the flowers will be encased in a protective coating.

7 | Allow the candle to cool and then decorate the second taper in the same way as the first to make a matching pair. The ball candle shown here has been decorated with a simple leaf design all round it.

TIP | Try using colored candles for this technique—pale pastels can look very pretty, and darker candles work if the plant material is strongly colored or very pale.

▶ Pressed flower candles can be made even more attractive by scenting the wax to complement the flowers. For example, use rose petals on rose-scented candles or ferns on pine-scented ones.

Stained Glass Candles

Stained glass candles have an outer coating of colored wax in a complex pattern that resembles millefiore, or stained glass. When the candle burns down, the colors are lit from within and the effect is extremely beautiful.

This is a relatively advanced technique for embellishing candles and one that is more easily achieved by commercial candlemakers. "Millefiore Canes" of wax with a complex pattern running right through their length are sliced thinly and applied to a base candle. This is then compressed in a mold for a smooth surface.

The technique given here is a simplified version of the commercial technique. Modeling wax is used for the canes as it is very pliable and easy to mold round the base candle after slicing. After the cane slices are applied to the base candle, it is dipped and then carved back to reveal the design.

Modeling wax is available in various colors but is sometimes limited to bright primaries. To obtain a larger color range, simply add dye to the colored modeling wax when it has melted. You will need to use a toning color to achieve the best results— blue wax can be dyed black or purple, yellow wax can be dyed green or orange, and so on.

☞

Dipping, pages 28–31
Votives, pages 139–141

YOU WILL NEED
Modeling wax—2 oz. each
   of black, magenta, and
   yellow
Three small dipping cans
   (pet food cans are
   ideal)
Large pan of boiling water
Two pieces of stiff wire,
   6 in. long
Sharp knife or blade
White ball candle
Wax glue
4 oz. uncolored dip and
   carve wax
Large dipping can

1 Melt the modeling wax and add dye if necessary. Fill the small dipping cans with boiling water and set in the large pan of boiling water over a heat source. Pour a different color of wax on the water in each. Bend a hook in the end of each wire to make it easier to hold. Allow the wax to cool to 160°F.

2 Dip each length of wire repeatedly into the yellow wax until it is about ¼ in. thick. The wire will pick up the wax in much the same way as a wick when dipping tapers. Allow the wax to cool for at least 30 seconds between each dip or it will not build up. This gives you plenty of time to dip both wires alternately, varying the colors of each if you wish.

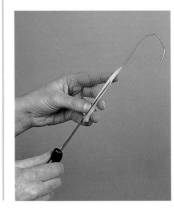

3 Allow the wax to cool a little. Score down the length of each cane several times all round with the tip of the knife to make grooves, at least four grooves down each cane. This will give the canes petal-like scallops.

5 Dip the canes into the magenta wax, building up a layer about 1/4 in. thick. When the canes are about 1/2 in. thick, score down the length of each as before. Then dip in the black wax again to define the grooves. Continue to build up the layers in the same way until the canes are about 3/4 in. thick, ending with a black layer.

7 Using a sharp knife, cut slices from each of the canes, about 1/16 in. thick. Rotate the canes a quarter turn after each slice to prevent them squashing and becoming distorted.

4 Dip the canes into the black wax about six times each. This will define the outside of the center of the petals. Be careful not to let the canes become too hot as they may slide off the wire before you want them to.

6 Allow the canes to cool until they can be handled without spoiling the surface. Ease each one off its wire. The wires should pull out quite easily, but be careful not to squeeze the canes.

8 Apply a little wax glue to the back of each slice and press it on the candle surface. You will be able to fit the slices together quite tightly; push them together further, distorting them to make them fit so that they cover as much of the candle as possible in a continuous layer of slices.

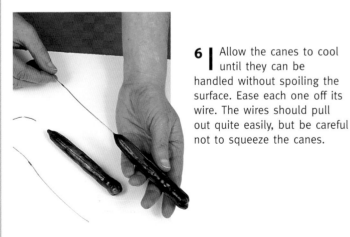

9 Work down the candle toward the base, cutting more slices as needed and pressing them on the candle with wax glue. You can use a hair drier to warm the slices if they are getting too cold to mold round the candle.

10 | When the candle is completely covered, smooth out any irregularities. You can cut half slices to fill any large gaps, or use slices cut from the smaller ends of the canes.

11 | Prepare the large dipping can for dipping with uncolored dip and carve wax. Dip the candle several times, making sure that any spaces between the slices are filled in.

12 | Use a sharp knife to pare back the coating of clear wax that has built up over the cane slices. This will give the candle a fairly smooth surface. If any of the slices protrude from the surface, also pare them back.

TIP | Instead of dipping the canes, two different colored sheets of modeling wax can be rolled up into a Swiss roll, then sliced to give spiral cane slices that look very attractive.

▼ You can vary the patterns and colors of stained glass candles by using different-colored modeling waxes and dipping patterns. The candle on the left has had spaces left between the cane slices for a lighter effect.

Stenciling

Stencils can be used on candles very successfully, and they are useful for creating repeat designs or attractive borders around a candle. The technique shown here uses a gold wax paste for stenciling, but you can use either acrylic paint or spray paint instead.

Stencils are available in an enormous variety of designs but they are rarely made in the small sizes needed for candles. An alternative is to use dolls' house stencils, which are available from dolls' house shops, but remember to buy flexible stencils so they will curve round a candle.

It is not difficult to make your own stencils. You can use waxed stencil paper or polyester acetate, or any flexible card. Choose a simple design that will not involve too much complicated cutting, and trace it on your stencil paper.

The paint used in this technique is a gold wax paste that adheres easily to the candle surface. If you use acrylic paint, you will need to apply a thin film to the candle first. Aerosol spray paint is another alternative, but you will need to mask the area around the candle as well as the rest of the candle itself. Work in a well-ventilated room if you use sprays.

Candles with straight sides or pillar candles are best for this technique, as it is almost impossible to attach a stencil to an egg or ball candle.

☞
**Painting,
pages 100–103**

YOU WILL NEED
Stenciling paper, card, or
  acetate
Pencil
Sharp craft knife or
  pyrography needle
Cutting mat or scrap
  cardboard
Dark blue pillar candle
Masking tape
Gold rub 'n buff paste or
  similar
Small piece of card
Paintbrush

1 Trace the design on the stencil paper and trim the paper to within 1 in. of the design all round. Then cut out the design with a sharp craft knife on a cutting mat. If you are using acetate and have a pyrography hot needle, you can use this to burn out the design instead, which is far easier. Remember to leave "bridges" of paper between the holes in the design or it will become too fragile.

2 Tape the stencil to the candle tightly with masking tape. Make sure that the top edge of the stencil is parallel to the top of the candle so that the design is kept straight.

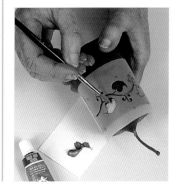

3 Squeeze some of the gold paste on a piece of scrap card. Paint through the holes in the stencil, using the brush. Avoid letting the brush bristles go under the stencil itself as this will smudge the design—paint along the lines of the cuts to avoid this.

4 Carefully remove the tape and lift the stencil from the candle surface. Clean the stencil with a rag and position it again, further round the candle and aligning it with the first pattern. Tape the stencil down again, being careful not to put tape over the newly painted design.

TEMPLATE
Enlarge this design with a photocopier if you wish. Trace the design on stencil paper and cut along the lines, removing all the blue areas.

5 Continue stenciling the design round the candle, being careful not to smudge areas that are already painted. You may have to adjust the design by spreading it out so that the motifs fit around the candle. Alternatively, paint part of a motif at the end to finish. Remove the stencil and use a fine brush to complete any parts of the design that have been missed.

▼ The finished candle shows how the stem in the final motif has been lengthened slightly to make the pattern fit around the candle. The green candle has been stenciled with a motif borrowed from a classical Greek vase.

6 Use the sharp craft knife to scrape away any rough edges of the design, but be careful not to damage the wax surface. Leave the candle to dry completely, then buff it with a soft cloth to bring up the shine on the gold paste.

Transfers

Applying transfers to candles is a very simple technique, but one that can produce delicate and professional results every time. White or cream candles are the best to use as most transfers are designed for use on a white background.

Transfers are available in a wonderful array of highly detailed designs and can be obtained from candlemakers' suppliers, egg crafting suppliers, or craft shops. The subject matter ranges from flowers, animals, birds, and butterflies to elegant borders, cameo portraits, seasonal holiday designs, and scenic paintings. There is usually a good deal of detail and the colors can be subtle and pastel through to luminous or bold.

The best candles to use are white or cream pillar candles or tapers. These give a relatively flat surface to which the transfer can be applied easily. Simple geometric shapes such as cube or pyramid candles are also suitable. Egg and round candles are less easy to use, as the flat transfer has to be curved to fit the surface, so choose smaller spot transfers for these shapes.

YOU WILL NEED
White pillar candle
Transfers
Saucer with water
Soft cloth

1 | Cut out your chosen transfers from the sheet with ¹/₂ in. of plain paper around the image. If you hold the sheet up to the light, you will be able to see where the rounded edges of the transfer come to, so do not cut into these. Make sure that the saucer is large enough for each transfer to fit into.

2 | Place the transfer into the saucer and press it down to submerge it in water. It will only take a minute or two to become loosened from the backing sheet. Check that the candle surface is free of dust and if necessary wipe it with a soft cloth.

3 | When you can see that the transfer is beginning to lift off the backing sheet, lift it from the water and lay it on the candle. Gently slide the transfer off the backing sheet, taking care that the edges do not fold under.

▶ The finished candle has an appealing simplicity. The small egg candle was decorated with a series of tiny spot-flower transfers.

4 | Use a soft cloth to pat the transfer on the candle surface, and mop away any excess water. You will find you can move the transfer about slightly to ensure it is perfectly upright. Leave the candle to dry overnight.

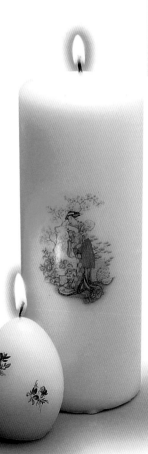

Whipping

If uncolored wax is stirred or whipped while it is cooling, it will become opaque and white, and will resemble frosty snow. It can then be applied to a candle surface to create textured candles.

This sequence makes a candle like a small snowball that is very attractive for Christmas, Thanksgiving, or other winter holiday decorations. The core candle is a small votive that is dipped into the whipped wax to cover it. If you use a larger core candle, it is easier to spread the whipped wax on the outside of a candle with a spatula instead.

You can make cheerful snowmen candles using this technique. Apply the whipped wax all over a short pillar candle, shaping it slightly to suggest a snowman's head and body. Use cut pieces of poured wax to add features and a scarf (see pages 60–63 for Sculpting).

The consistency of whipped wax can be varied by how much you whip it. Wax that has been whipped with a wire whisk will be fluffier and lighter than wax that has been stirred with a fork.

The wax used in this sequence was uncolored, but you could add chalky white candle dye for a more opaque result. You can also use dyed wax of any color but remember that it will become much paler when whipped. This type of wax is used for novelty candles that simulate ice cream or sundaes. It is scooped up with a spoon or an ice cream scoop and pressed into a glass or an ice cream cone. A primed wick is then inserted into a hole made with a wicking needle while the wax is still soft.

Whipped candles can be further embellished using spangles, beads, glitter, or dripping.

YOU WILL NEED
8 oz. uncolored paraffin wax
Stearin (10% of wax weight)
Container for the candle
Fork for whipping
Core candle—a small votive candle with a long wick is ideal
Chopping board or similar smooth surface

1 Heat the paraffin wax with the Stearin until it is melted. Pour the wax into the container and leave until it begins to cool. The wax will first set on the top and round the sides and bottom of the container.

2 Scrape the set wax off the edges of the container with the fork and combine it with the molten wax in the middle. You will need to keep the wax moving, stirring the cooled wax into the soft wax.

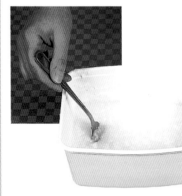

3 After some time of continuous stirring, the wax will begin to look like white scrambled egg. Still keep it moving— otherwise some areas will become set before you are ready to apply the wax to the candle.

4 Take the small votive candle and hold it by the wick. Place the candle into the wax and use the fork to cover it completely with wax until it is buried.

5 | Leave the core candle in the wax for about 30 seconds so that it softens and the whipped wax adheres to it. Keep hold of the candle by the wick so that you can remove it easily.

7 | Drop the candle from a height of about 4 in. on a smooth surface to flatten the bottom. The whipped wax will still be soft enough to compress into a sturdy base on the bottom of the candle. Leave it to cool for a minute or two, remove it from the surface, and set aside to cool thoroughly.

8 | The finished candle can be left plain, or decorated further. To add glitter, roll the candle in glue and then on a sheet of paper scattered with glitter. Sequins can also be glued on the candle, and beads, threaded on pins and stuck into the candle, add sparkles of light.

▼ Whipped candles have a lovely rough texture that catches the light from the candle flame. The glitter gives the effect of frosty snow.

6 | Lift the candle out of the wax by the wick and knock off any loose wax with the fork. Scrape off the excess wax to form a pleasing shape.

Wrapping

Candles can be wrapped in many different ways to create novelty gifts and decorations. Here, a stocky pillar candle has been wrapped with bamboo and raffia for a South Sea Island look.

Wrapped candles should normally be considered as decorations as it is important to remove the wrapping before burning the candle to avoid a fire risk. One alternative to this is to place the candle in a snug-fitting glass or jar, and wrap the outside of that. The candle can then be burned safely as the wrapping material is kept away from the flame.

You can be highly imaginative as to the materials you use to wrap your candles and the list below will give you some ideas. Try to think in terms of themes when wrapping, and combine materials that go naturally together.

You can use the color of the candle to enhance the final effect. For example, a bright saffron yellow candle looks stunning wrapped with dried red chillies and bay leaves, while a delicate, pale pink candle combines well with cinnamon sticks and lavender.

OTHER WRAPPINGS
- Fall leaves
- Twigs or bark
- Dried orange or lemon slices
- Dried apple or pear slices
- Handmade paper and lace
- Fresh herbs and jute string
- Fresh flowers, leaves, and ribbon
- Holly leaves and silver thread
- Cinnamon sticks
- Dried chillies
- Ears of wheat or barley

YOU WILL NEED
Short, honey-brown pillar candle
Thin bamboo garden cane
Small hacksaw
Cutting surface
Wax glue and spatula
Raffia
Scissors

1 Measure the bamboo against the height of the candle to find the length required. The bamboo lengths must be the same height as the straight sides of the candle so that the pointed top of the candle will appear above the wrapping.

2 Cut off the length of bamboo with the hacksaw. Cut halfway through from each side and snap the cane across the cuts. Use this length to measure the other lengths and cut enough bamboo to go round the candle.

3 Scrape up some wax glue on the spatula and apply tiny dabs to a bamboo length at both ends and in the center. You may find it easier to use the wax glue if you leave it in a warm place for a while first.

4 | Press the glued side of the bamboo on the candle, making sure that it is absolutely upright. Repeat this for the next cane and continue round the candle. It is important that the canes do not protrude beyond the base of the candle or it will not stand straight.

5 | When you have worked all round the candle, you will need to adjust the spacing between the last few canes so that they fit neatly and there are no large gaps.

6 | Double a length of raffia and tie it in a double knot round the center of the candle and the bamboo canes. Trim the ends of the knot to about 1 in.

▼ The muted colors of the bamboo-wrapped candle complement its honey-scented beeswax. The red candle has been wrapped with dried apple slices and cinnamon sticks. The raffia binding makes a perfect finishing touch and secures the wrappings.

DISPLAY TECHNIQUES

It is only when candles are lit
that they display their full
glory: the flicker of the flame,
the illumination of the wax
itself, and the glow of light that
creates a special atmosphere.
This section shows you how to
enhance these wonderful
qualities by using a rich variety
of displaying techniques.

Candleholders with Papier Mâché

This technique shows you how to make simple, but striking candleholders for your candles out of papier mâché. These can then be finished in many different ways, two of which are given here.

Papier mâché is an ideal material for making candleholders: it is cheap, readily available, and easy to model. The technique shown here uses a simple card base to give the basic shape of the candleholder, which is built up around a store-bought candle cup. An alternative to the candle cup is to use a metal bottle screw cap, but you could also simply build up the papier mâché around the base of the candle you wish to use.

Papier mâché can be made at home from newspaper and glue, and a recipe is given here. Alternatively, use one of the proprietary quick-setting modeling materials that are similar to papier mâché and just require the addition of water. If you prefer, you could use air-drying modeling clay instead—the following instructions will work well for any of these materials.

INSTRUCTIONS FOR MAKING 1³/₄ PINTS PAPIER MÂCHÉ

YOU WILL NEED
Four large sheets of newspaper
3¹/₂ pints of water
Large saucepan
Sieve
Two tablespoons PVA glue
Two tablespoons wallpaper paste
Bowl

1 Tear the newspaper into small pieces and soak in the water overnight.
2 Put the mixture in a large saucepan and boil it, stirring until the paper disintegrates. Whisk the mixture until it is soft and pulpy.
3 Spoon the pulp into the sieve and squeeze out the excess water.
4 Place in a bowl and stir in the glue and wallpaper paste.

STAR CANDLEHOLDER
Medieval blue and gold ceiling designs were the inspiration for this sparkling candleholder decorated with acrylic paint. Further ideas are imitation gold leaf, glass paint relief outliner, and pressed flowers.

1 Draw a simple six-pointed star, 6 in. across, on the card and use the craft knife and a straight edge to cut out the shape.

YOU WILL NEED
Strong mounting card
Tracing paper and pencil
Heavy-duty craft knife
Cutting board
Straight edge or metal ruler
Candle cup
PVA glue
Papier mâché (see below left) or proprietary modeling material
Knife
Sandpaper
Acrylic paint—blue, white
Saucer for mixing
Water pot
Paintbrush
Gold paint

2 Squeeze some PVA glue into the center of the card star and press the candle cup on the glue to secure it. Leave it to dry. This will serve as a guide as to the height of the candleholder and make modeling the star easier.

3 Spoon the papier mâché on the star and use your fingers to pack it around the candle cup. Continue to spoon on papier mâché and build up the star to the height of the top of the candle cup, curving it down to the ends of the points of the star.

4 Use the knife to refine the shape, neatening all the edges. Make grooves between the points running up to the candle cup for an attractive shape. Leave the papier mâché to dry in a warm place overnight, or place it in a cool oven at 150°F for several hours to speed up the drying process.

5 When the star is completely dry, sand the surface to remove any lumps or protrusions. You can continue to sand until the surface is quite smooth or leave it slightly textured.

6 Mix some white acrylic paint into the blue to make a shade of mid-blue. Paint the star all over, working the paint into any crevices so that it covers it completely. Leave to dry.

7 Use the gold paint to paint stars on the candleholder. You can emphasize the points with gold as well and paint smaller stars and dots between the larger stars to resemble a medieval ceiling decoration.

▼ The finished candleholder provides a secure base for a burning candle. You could also try making a smaller version for tiny tapers, and display them in a group as a galaxy of stars for a table centerpiece.

POLYMER CLAY MOSAIC CANDLEHOLDER

Polymer clay, or home-baked modeling clay, is the perfect material for creating mosaics. This design is inspired by Roman mosaic floors. The pink and olive-green clays used are granite-effect clays but you could use plain clay instead. If the polymer clay is stiff, knead it until it becomes soft and pliable. Some clays can be used straight from the packet. Follow the manufacturers' instructions for baking temperatures and times. The oven temperatures needed to bake polymer clay will not harm the papier mâché base.

YOU WILL NEED
PVA glue and spreader
Papier mâché candleholder in the shape of a square (see pages 118–119)
Smooth rolling pin or glass bottle
Two strips of wood or card, about ¹/₁₆ in. thick
Smooth board or surface
Pencil
Craft knife with a curved blade
Polymer clay—white, black, olive-green granite-effect, pink granite-effect

1 | Spread a thin coat of glue all round the candle cup in the center of the candleholder. This is to help the polymer clay stick to the surface of the papier mâché. It does not matter if it dries, it will still provide a key.

2 | Roll out the black polymer clay between the wood or card strips. Your rolling pin should rest on the card strips while the clay is rolled out between them. This will ensure that the clay sheet is rolled to a uniform thickness.

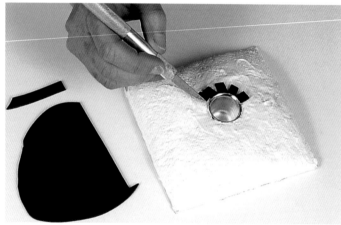

3 | Cut a strip of clay from the black sheet, about ¹/₄ in. wide. Press it lightly on your board so that it sticks. Cut ¹/₄ in. squares from the strip. As you cut each square, scoop it up on the blade of your knife—it should stick to the blade as the clay is slightly tacky. A curved blade makes this much easier to do.

4 | Lift the square on the blade into position on the candleholder. This way, you do not have to touch the clay squares with your hands, which would distort them, and you can work very quickly. Use the blade to push the squares into place if necessary. Work around the candle cup, radiating the squares out from it.

5 | When the central circle is complete, draw pencil lines across the candleholder to divide it into nine large squares. These lines will guide you as you apply the polymer clay squares. Spread glue along one of the central lines and cut more black squares to apply as before, working along the line and keeping the squares lined up and straight.

6 | Continue with the other lines, applying glue and pressing on the black squares. You will find that you can work quite quickly once you have practiced applying each square with the knife blade. Finish the center sections first.

7 | Roll out some white, pink and olive-green clay in the same way. Spread glue inside a section outlined with black squares and apply a row of white squares round the edge. Build up a checkerboard of green and black in the center, still keeping all the squares aligned in the same way. Cut triangles of pink clay and fill in the spaces around the central ring.

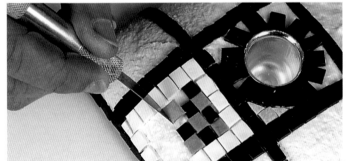

8 | Finish the design and apply a black row all round the base of the candleholder. Fill in any gaps in the central ring with wedges of black clay. Use a small rolling pin or bottle to roll over the design, flattening it slightly and pressing the mosaic squares together. Bake in the oven at 265°F for about 30 minutes (or follow the instructions on the pack) and leave to cool.

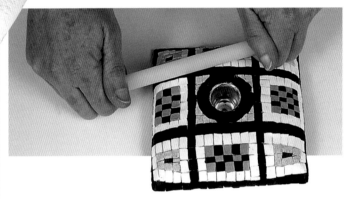

▼ The bold geometric patterns of the mosaic give the finished candleholder a striking appearance. Use a taper that matches one of the clay colors to complete the effect.

Candleholder with Salt Dough

Salt dough is a wonderful medium for making objects for the home. The subtle colors of the baked dough have a lovely homely feel. Here it is used to make simple candleholders that will enhance any table setting or windowsill.

Salt dough is a simple flour and water dough with a high proportion of salt. The dough is easy to shape, and after baking hard and varnishing will keep for long periods of time. When you have mixed the dough, you can keep it fresh for several days wrapped in cling film in a cool place. While you are working with the dough, keep it in a bowl covered with plastic wrap or it will dry out. If it becomes dry, just knead it with damp hands to moisten it; if it is too wet, add a little flour.

The design shown here uses simple sculpted shells to decorate a ring candleholder but there are many other designs you could model. Try using cookie or canapé cutters to cut out shapes in the dough. Cake decorating cutters can also be used for leaves and flowers. You could also model novelty candleholders in the shape of animals—a turtle carrying a candle in its back, or small fish pressed onto the central ring for a centerpiece for a fish supper.

Salt dough can be colored after baking with watercolor or acrylic paints. It is essential to varnish the piece with several coats of matte or gloss varnish whether you have painted it or not. This seals the surface and prevents deterioration.

YOU WILL NEED
Two cups plain flour
One cup fine salt
Mixing bowl
Water
Plastic wrap
Ceramic tile or foil-lined cookie sheet
Candle
Sharp knife
Polyurethane varnish and brush

1 Put the flour and salt into the mixing bowl and stir thoroughly. Add water, a little at a time and stir to make a dough. Be careful not to add too much water, or the mixture will become sticky.

2 Knead the dough on a work surface until it is smooth and elastic. Wrap it in plastic wrap and place it in the refrigerator for 30 minutes to rest before using.

3 Stand the candle upright in the center of the tile. Roll out a log of the dough, long enough to wrap round the base of the candle. Trim the log to length and use a little water to moisten the ends of the dough before pressing them together.

4 To make the cockleshells, roll out a log of clay and cut four equal lengths. Form each into a ball of dough and press into a little dome on the board. Pinch one end to narrow it and use your knife to make cuts radiating out from the pinched end to the broad end.

7 | When the candleholder is finished, remove the candle. Bake the candleholder in a cool oven on 160°F for 30 minutes, then raise the temperature to about 212°F and bake until the holder is an even golden color all over and completely hard. This may take at least two hours.

5 | Moisten the base ring with a little water and press the cockleshell on it. Repeat to make three more cockleshells and press them round the base ring with the broad end towards the candle.

6 | For the spiral shells, cut equal lengths as before and form each into a long thin log of dough with a pointed end. Twirl this into a spiral, starting at the broad end and spiraling upwards to the pointed end. Moisten the base ring and press a spiral shell into each space between the cockles.

8 | When the candleholder is cool, varnish with several coats of polyurethane varnish. Do not forget to varnish the underside of the holder as any unvarnished areas will become damp and deteriorate.

▼ The finished holder will hold a taper very securely. The second candleholder is made in the same way, but is decorated with modeled flowers and leaves.

Candlepots

Ordinary terracotta flowerpots are perfect containers for making attractive candleholders. They can either be filled with fresh or dried flowers, as here, or the candle can be placed inside the decorated pot.

Florist's foam is available in two kinds for either dried or fresh flower arranging and can be put to excellent use for a candle and flower arrangement in a flowerpot. The candle is fixed securely in the foam and then the flowers are arranged around it. If you use dried flowers, as here, the arrangement is permanent, but fresh flowers are a glorious alternative for a special occasion. For a fresh arrangement, use the wet kind of florist's foam and line the flowerpot with plastic to avoid spills.

There are many other ways that you can decorate candlepots. If you fill the pot with foam but trim it to just below the rim of the pot, you can cover the surface around the candle with all sorts of materials. Pebbles, glass nuggets, decorated Easter eggs, pine cones, or candy and sweets all make exciting and original displays for various occasions.

If you use any form of flammable material with your candlepots, especially dried flowers or plant material, you should not leave them unattended when burning.

☞
Dried flowers, pages 104–105
Wrapping, pages 114–115

YOU WILL NEED
5 in. terracotta flowerpot
Florist's dry foam—small cylinder to fit the pot or a block
Sharp knife
Candle
Stiff wire
Pliers
Masking tape
Fine florist's wire
Selection of dried flowers
Raffia
Glue

1 Cut the florist's foam cylinder at an angle all round the base so that it will fit tightly into the flowerpot with about 1 in. protruding above the rim.

2 Place the foam in the flowerpot and trim the top at an angle so it makes a smooth dome. This type of foam cuts very easily with a sharp knife.

3 Cut two lengths of wire, each about 4 in. long, and bend them into a "U" shape. Tape one on either side of the candle with the two prongs held straight down. This will provide a firm anchorage for the candle in the foam.

4 Hold the candle above the center of the foam and push it down so that the wires pierce into the foam and are driven right down vertically.

5 Cut some sprays of flowers. If their stems are too fragile to press into the foam, make small bunches and wind fine green florist's wire around the stems to strengthen them, leaving the ends of the wire pointing downwards so that you can push the wire into the foam.

6 The first sprays should be pushed into the sides of the foam at an upward angle so that they slope down and partly cover the rim of the pot. Build up the sprays, pushing them into the exposed foam and packing them fairly tightly for an attractive result.

7 When you have covered the foam with sprays, push in a few attractive flowers such as dried roses to complete the arrangement. Dried fern or grass can be added as well but keep it away from the candle as it will burn very easily.

8 Finally tie a bow of raffia around the pot. You may need to use a little glue to keep the raffia from sliding down the sides of the pot.

TIP When one candle has burnt down, you can tape wire prongs to another to replace it so that your candlepot lasts indefinitely.

▼ The combination of terracotta, white wax, and dried flowers is particularly pleasing. Try making candlepots as matching pairs for an al fresco dinner table. Large candlepots with fresh flowers and pillar candles look stunning lining the steps down to a deck or garden for a special occasion.

Cuffs

Candle cuffs are traditionally made of metal or glass and are placed around the base of the candle to catch any drips of wax. They can be plain or highly decorated. This technique shows you how to make cuffs for your candles using embossed copper or brass sheet.

Brass and copper metal sheet for embossing is available from craft shops. It can be cut easily with a pair of old scissors and the embossing technique is no more difficult than making simple tracings. The results are extremely effective and the embossed surfaces of the metal catch the candlelight for a stunning display. If the cuffs are bent and curved, as shown here, the result resembles antique metalwork.

The ball tool used here can be purchased from craft shops or sculpting suppliers, but you could use any blunt instrument instead. A dried-out ball-point pen is ideal for finer lines. Practice using the tools on scraps of metal sheet first. When you draw with the embossing tool, you are making a shallow impression in the brass. This side will then become the underside and the embossing will show through as attractive raised designs on the upper side.

Brass sheet should be cleaned with very fine wire wool before embossing. Test a piece of wire wool first to see if it is fine enough—it should polish the sheet and leave no scratches.

☞
Sconces, pages 136–138

YOU WILL NEED
Brass embossing sheet
Fine wire wool, or metal polish and a rag
Pencil and tracing paper
Masking tape (optional)
Old pair of scissors
Cloth
Thick cardboard
Ball tool
White spirit
Polyurethane varnish and brush

1 Polish the brass sheet thoroughly with a small piece of wire wool. You should be able to give the sheet a mirror finish.

2 Trace the template on tracing paper. Check that the inner circle is just larger than the diameter of the candles you intend to use, and enlarge if necessary. Lay the tracing over the brass sheet, securing it with masking tape if necessary. Trace the design outline on the sheet, pressing just hard enough to make a light mark on the brass.

3 Cut out the design, using an old pair of scissors as the sheet may blunt them. As you cut, be careful of the sharp edges of the sheet.

4 Lay the cuff on a soft cloth and use the point of the scissors to pierce a hole in the center. Insert the point of the scissors into the hole and cut out the inner circle of the cuff.

5 Lay the cuff on the thick cardboard and press firmly as you draw along the lines of the design with the ball tool. The cardboard will give slightly as you draw and produce an attractive embossed line on the other side. Draw all round the edges, about ¹/₁₆ in. from the edge itself. This will give the effect of a rolled and thicker edge on the upper side.

6 Turn the cuff over and draw between the raised lines to emphasize them. This will accentuate the design and make the light catch the surfaces more effectively.

7 To give the cuff a concertina effect, bend it across the center and along the lines of the design. You will need to make three upward folds alternating with three downward folds. Fold the cuff between your fingers and be careful not to fold too far back—the folds should be quite gentle.

8 Wipe over the cuff with mineral spirits to remove fingerprints or grease. Varnish with two coats of varnish. If you want an antique look to your cuff, leave it to tarnish slightly for a few weeks before varnishing. You can leave cuffs unvarnished, but it is difficult to polish them with metal polish without spoiling the embossing.

TIP It is fun designing your own cuffs. Draw a circle of about 3 in. diameter with a pair of compasses, and draw another circle inside, just larger than the diameter of your candle. Decorate the cuffs with simple motifs or random geometric lines, or pierce holes in the edge of the cuff and suspend beads or charms from the holes with fine jewelry wire.

▼ Embossed brass cuffs catch the light and will turn the most ordinary candle into something special. To use the cuffs, place the candle into its candlestick and simply drop the cuff over it to rest at the base of the candle.

TEMPLATE
Enlarge the template with a photocopier so that the inner circle is just larger than your candle's diameter.

Ice Bowl Holder for Floating Candles

There is something magical about the combination of candlelight and water and floating candles provide this glorious effect. The ice bowl container shown here adds a truly remarkable sparkle.

It is fun to be imaginative when choosing a container for your floating candles. Colorful pottery bowls go well with brightly colored candles while glass and crystal look beautiful with pastel and white candles. You can use any watertight container for displaying floating candles, from old tin cans to silver bowls, champagne buckets to a large shell. Grouped containers look particularly effective, such as a series of tall, frosted drinking glasses each holding a single, floating candle.

The water in the container can be left plain or have petals and leaves floated on the surface. A few whole flowers, such as large tea roses or water lilies, can look stunning. Glass nuggets in the bottom of the bowl are a well-known addition, but consider using shells, large beads, coins, or a collection of marbles.

The ice bowl shown here forms an attractive and unusual container for floating candles. Marigolds and fir sprays are used for the inclusions but there are many alternatives.

☞
Inclusions, pages 94–95

YOU WILL NEED
Large round plastic bowl (ice cream container or similar)
Jug of water
Freezer—or freezing temperatures outside
Small plastic or china bowl, about 2 in. less in diameter than the large bowl
Pebbles or weights
Ice cubes (optional)
Flowers—marigolds and sprays of pine
Glass dish

1 Pour about ½ in. of water into the bottom of the large bowl. Freeze for at least two hours, keeping it as level as possible, to give a thick layer of ice. This forms the base of the ice bowl.

2 Fill the smaller bowl with pebbles or weights and place centrally into the large bowl, on top of the ice layer. If it slides on the ice, push a few small ice cubes down between the bowls to wedge it in place.

3 Push the flowers and leaves into the space between the bowls, arranging them evenly. You may need to pull the petals off larger flowers to make them fit in the available space.

4 Pour water into the space between the bowls, filling it to about ½ in. from the top. The plant material may try to float so wedge it down with more leaves. Freeze the bowls on a level surface for several hours or overnight until the water is completely frozen.

5 Lift the smaller bowl out of the larger one. If it is held fast by the ice, tip out the pebbles and fill it with hot water for a few minutes until you can release it.

6 Leave the ice bowl, still in the outer bowl, in the freezer until just before you need it. Remove it from the freezer and ease the ice bowl out of the large bowl. The flexible plastic should make it easy to release but if necessary hold it in hot water for a few moments. Place the ice bowl in a glass dish to catch melted water.

7 The flowers and leaves should be clearly visible through the ice. To use the bowl, fill it with chilled water and place the floating candles on the surface. The bowl will begin to melt after a while but the glass dish will catch the water. To prolong the ice bowl's life, pack ice cubes tightly around it in the dish.

▼ When the floating candles are lit, the flowers and leaves are illuminated in a sparkle of ice. You could also add fresh fruit to your ice bowl such as slices of oranges and lemons, strawberries and their leaves, or small clusters of redcurrants.

Natural Holders

Pumpkin lanterns at Halloween are familiar to everyone, but there are many other natural containers that you can use to display your candles. In the techniques shown here, oranges are transformed into glowing balls of light and dainty shells hold slim tapers.

Many different fruits and vegetables can be hollowed out to make candleholders. Beside the ubiquitous pumpkin, Halloween lanterns are traditionally made with turnips or marrows and, in warmer climates, gourds and melons. Citrus fruits, such as lemons, grapefruit, and large limes, have leathery skins and make ideal candleholders. A pyramid of oranges and lemons containing tea lights makes a beautiful table centerpiece. Other ideas using natural objects for displaying candles are:
• Coconut shells—you can gild the inside with metal leaf or gold paint, and use them as containers for votives.
• Oyster or cockleshells—fill with wax and insert a wick for original container candles.
• Log of wood with the bark still on—halve the log lengthways to provide a sturdy base and drill holes to hold candles. These make particularly attractive Christmas candleholders when decorated with twined holly and ivy.

ORANGE VOTIVES

In the technique shown here, an orange is hollowed out and a small tea light set inside. The candlelight glows through the peel and if this is further embellished with carved lines, it makes a beautiful holder.

YOU WILL NEED
Orange
Red felt-tip pen
Chopping board
Lino-cutting tool
Sharp vegetable knife
Bowl
Spoon
Kitchen scissors
Tea light

1 Use the pen to sketch your design on the orange. Red shows up well but will not be visible after the orange is carved. The best designs are simple geometric zigzags and crosses or curving scrolls. Leave the top ½ in. of the orange undecorated as it will be cut off.

2 Use the lino-cutting tool to gouge out the design along your pen marks. Make a shallow groove first and then deepen it if necessary.

3 When the design is completed all round, cut off the top of the orange. It is easier to carve the design before cutting or hollowing out the fruit because it will be firmer when still whole. Cut round inside the orange flesh with your knife, freeing it from the sides. Be careful not to cut through the skin as this will weaken it as a holder.

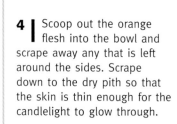

4 Scoop out the orange flesh into the bowl and scrape away any that is left around the sides. Scrape down to the dry pith so that the skin is thin enough for the candlelight to glow through.

5 | Snip round the top of the orange with the scissors to make a zigzag pattern. Also use the scissors to snip away any remaining membrane inside the orange, as it would get in the way of the candle flame.

6 | Place a tea light inside the orange. You can make a series of orange candleholders with different designs to display along a mantelpiece or windowsill. The oranges will last for a few days, and then will begin to wrinkle and dry out. Store them in a freezer until they are needed.

SHELL CANDLEHOLDERS

The second technique uses polymer clay to stabilize small shells, which then have a thin taper set into them with wax. These look particularly effective when arranged in groups of different kinds of shell.

2 | Heat some paraffin wax until melted, and transfer to a small jug. Then place the base of a small taper into the shell and pour wax around the base, filling up the shell to hold the candle firmly. Hold the candle in position until the wax has set; this should take only a minute or two.

YOU WILL NEED
Ceramic tile or cookie sheet
White polymer clay
Shells—with holes large enough to take candles
Superglue (cyanoacrylate glue)
Small tapers
2–3 oz. paraffin wax

1 | Press down a ½ in. ball of polymer clay on the tile to form a disc. Press a shell on the clay disc so that it is held upright. Bake the shell and clay on the tile for 20–30 minutes at 265°F, or at the temperature recommended by the manufacturer. When cool, separate clay and shell and glue them back together for security.

▼ The lit orange candleholders make a glorious glow, especially when grouped together. The simple shell holders can also be displayed nestled in a bowl of pebbles—tuck a few small flowers among them for a charming natural effect.

Recycling—Jars, Bottles, and Tins

Recycled jars and tins make extremely successful containers for displaying candles, as the following techniques demonstrate. Glass paints transform ordinary jelly jars into rainbow lanterns while perforated tins glow like fairy lights in the dark.

There are so many types of glass jars, bottles, and containers that you need never be at a loss to find something to decorate for a candleholder. Painted with brilliantly colored transparent glass paints, the candle inside will light up the glass like a stained glass window. Large preserving jars, jelly jars of every shape, baby food jars, custard cups—the selection is enormous. Then there are bottles, which come in many different colors of glass. To display candles in bottles, soften the base of the candle in hot water until you can press it into the top of the bottle.

Glass paints and outliners are available at most craft shops and besides the wonderful color range, there is a choice of water-based or faster-drying spirit-based paints. The traditional method shown here is to draw in the outline of the design with relief outliner and fill in the areas between with glass paint. However, rules are made to be broken and you can paint graded areas of paint over your jar and when it is dry draw in a design with the relief outliner. Glass paint colors can be mixed to give further colors and a medium is provided to dilute the colors to make pastel shades.

YOU WILL NEED
Clean jelly jar
Paper and felt-tip pen
Scissors
Denatured alcohol
Glass relief outliner in
    black
Glass paints in several
    colors
Paintbrush
Small containers for mixing
Kitchen paper or tissues

PAINTED GLASS JARS AND BOTTLES

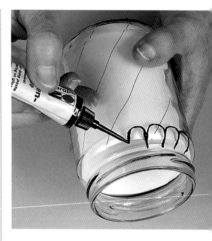

1 Select a jar or bottle and wash it thoroughly in hot, soapy water removing any traces of the label. Cut a piece of white paper to fit inside the jar and draw your design on it with the pen. Form the paper into a tube and push into the jar. Open it out inside the jar so that you can see the design through the glass.

2 Wipe over the outside of the jar with denatured alcohol to de-grease the surface. After you have done this, avoid touching the surface of the jar as much as possible.

3 Draw in the outlines of the design with the relief outliner, using the pen lines visible inside the jar as guidelines. It is easiest to draw regular lines with an outliner if you pull it toward you for a stroke, rather like icing a cake.

4 Continue round the jar. Take care that you do not smudge earlier lines with your hand as you turn the jar—it might be easier to let one side dry before drawing the lines on the other side.

5 Leave the outliner to dry for several hours or overnight. Support the jar on kitchen paper to prevent it rolling. Paint in the areas between the outlines with the glass paints. The paint flows on easily but needs to be applied sparingly. Do not go over areas that you have already painted as this will spoil the shiny finish.

6 Allow each section to dry for a few minutes before moving on to the next. Leave the first side of the jar to dry completely before painting the other or the paint may drip badly. Small foil dishes are useful for mixing colors in.

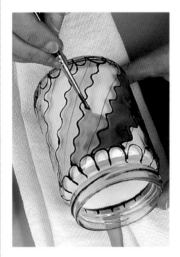

7 When the main design is dry, paint round the edges right up to the top of the jar. Leave it to dry thoroughly and fix a candle inside (see Tip Box). To hang the jar, twist wire firmly around the top and attach a loop handle of wire to this.

TIP To place a candle in the jar, heat the candle base with a match to melt it, then quickly press it into the bottom of the jar so that it sticks fast. Another way to secure candles in jars is to put a 1–2 in. deep layer of sand in the bottom of the jar and stand the candle in that.

▼ Votive flames light up the jewel colors of these jars, while a simple beer bottle is transformed into an opulent candlestick. The red jar was painted with stripes of red, pink, and yellow glass paint, and then a flowing dragon design was drawn on with gold outliner.

TIN CANS

Cans can be transformed into gleaming candle lanterns with the help of a hammer and nail. The best cans to choose are those with a shiny exterior. Soak off any labels in hot, soapy water. Many cans have ridges, which adds to the textural effect. Cans come in many sizes and you can make large lanterns out of economy-size cans or tiny lanterns for tea lights.

In the technique shown here, the tin is filled with water and frozen so that the ice inside it supports it when you hammer the holes. Choose the nail you use to hammer the holes carefully—the point will affect the shape of the holes you make. You could also vary the size of the nail and use a larger one for the outlines and a smaller nail for making the spirals or crosses.

Try painting the tins with different shades of glass paints for a more colorful effect.

YOU WILL NEED
Clean can with label
  removed
Freezer
Old towel
Hammer
Large nail
Galvanized wire
Pliers

1 Fill the can with water, right up to the top, and freeze overnight. Place the towel on a firm surface. Lay the tin (which is now full of solid ice) on its side on the towel.

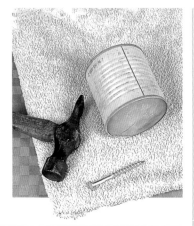

2 Hold the point of the nail vertically on the can and hammer with several hard bangs to make a hole. The ice will support the sides of the can and prevent them bending, and you should be able to make a neat hole. Make more holes, working round the can in a line and rotating it as you work so that the place where you hammer each hole is uppermost. This prevents the nail from skidding off the can.

3 Hammer a design of holes in the center of the can on each side. Use simple shapes such as crosses and spirals that you can hammer out easily.

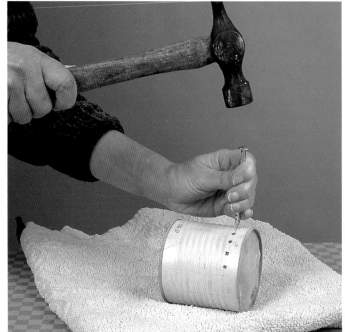

4 When the holes are done, leave the can standing in a bowl to thaw out the ice. To make the hanger, cut three lengths of wire, each 12 in. long. Push one end of each through a hole in the top of the tin, bend it up, and twist it around itself to secure. The wires need to be evenly spaced for the tin to hang straight.

5 | Gather all three wires together at the top and twist them round themselves to join them. You may have to use two pairs of pliers to do this if the wire is stiff.

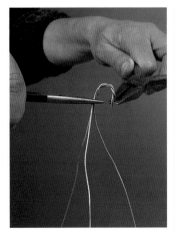

6 | Bend over the top of the twisted wires into a large hook. This can be hung over branches in trees for an outdoor display or along a wire. Secure a candle inside in the same way as for the jars on page 33. Remember that the candle will give out considerable heat when lit so avoid letting inflammable material overhang the lantern.

▶ When the candle is lit, the nail holes shine out like stars and a glow emerges from the top of the can. The cans look beautiful hanging in trees around the garden on a summer's night. The candles inside are well sheltered from the wind, and will burn for several hours.

Sconces

Sconces are candleholders that are hung on walls. They are often made of brass and silver to reflect the light of the candle flame. This simple version, made with embossed copper sheet, could rival any costly antique sconce.

At its most simple, a sconce is a ledge for holding candles, combined with an upright back to hang it on the wall. The basic design given here is of two pieces of wood, joined into a little shelf, and clad with embossed copper sheet and a tiny mirror to add to the reflection. The embossed design is inspired by Celtic spirals found in Iron Age metalwork. Taper or pillar candles are used traditionally with sconces; try grouping several small tapers on the ledge for a medieval look.

Copper sheet is embossed in exactly the same way as brass sheet. See the detailed instructions for embossing brass sheet on pages 126–127. Alternatively, you could paint the wood with folk art designs, or cover it with gold leaf or a polymer clay mosaic.

☞
**Gold leaf, pages 90–91
Polymer clay mosaic
candleholder, page 120**

YOU WILL NEED
Two pieces of 1/4 in. thick
   plywood: 5 x 3 3/4 in.
   and 5 x 8 in.
Sand paper
Brass picture-hanging loop
3/16 in. tacks
Wood glue
3/8 in. nails
Brick for support
Hammer
Copper embossing sheet
Metal polish and a rag
Pencil and tracing paper
Old pair of scissors
Thick cardboard
Ball tool
Small oval mirror, 2 x 1 1/2 in.
Superglue (cyanoacrylate
   glue)
Mineral spirits
Polyurethane varnish and
   brush

1 Sand the edges of the wood pieces to remove any rough edges. Tack the picture-hanging loop to the top center of the larger piece of wood using the hammer and tacks.

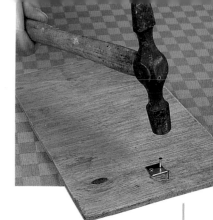

2 Apply wood glue to the back edge of the smaller piece of wood. Using the brick as support, nail the bottom front of the larger piece of wood to the back edge of the smaller piece.

3 Clean the copper sheet with a rag dipped in metal polish. Trace the design for the sconce top design on the tracing paper. Then lay the tracing paper on the copper sheet and draw around the outside line with a pencil, pressing slightly to make a visible mark.

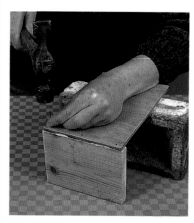

4 Cut out the sconce top with an old pair of scissors. The cut edges of the copper are very sharp so handle it with great care.

5 Place the tracing on the cutout copper sheet. Using the thick cardboard as a work surface, draw lightly over the inside lines of the design with a pencil, pressing just hard enough to leave a mark on the copper.

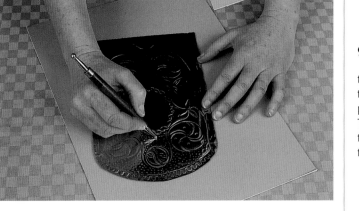

6 Remove the tracing. Use the ball tool to draw over the design, pressing firmly to make an even impression. This side will become the back of the piece, with the design showing as a raised embossing on the other side. If you impress a line just inside the edge of the sheet it will roll the edge and make it look like thicker metal from the other side.

7 When you have completed the design, turn the sheet over and impress between the raised lines with the ball tool. This will accentuate the relief and produce a more opulent and solid effect.

8 Place the embossed copper sheet on the wooden sconce back and fold the edges back around the wood to make a snug fit. Try to bend the copper sheet accurately the first time, because mistakes are difficult to smooth out.

9 Slide the metal sheet up and apply glue to the wood surface. Slide the sheet back down and press lightly into place. The glue will take some time to dry but it will hold the sheet in place.

10 To cover the sconce base, stand the sconce upright on a piece of copper sheet and mark all around it, allowing ½ in. extra on the two short and one long side. Cut out the shape and glue it to the wooden sconce base, turning the edges under to neaten them.

11 | Glue the mirror into the center of the sconce back with superglue. Wipe over the copper with mineral spirits, and paint it with two coats of polyurethane varnish. The varnish will prevent the copper from tarnishing.

12 | Melt the base of a candle with a match and allow it to drip on the sconce base to make a small pool of wax. Quickly press the candle firmly down on the base. Make sure it is firmly in place before lighting.

TIP | The upper areas of the sconce are embossed with a texture of small dots impressed with the ball tool. Adding texture in this way to plain areas will give the piece more reflective surfaces to shine in the candlelight.

▼ The warm glow of copper looks particularly beautiful by candlelight as the finished sconce shows. Try making a pair of matching sconces to hang on either side of a doorway or fireplace.

TEMPLATE
Enlarge this template with a photocopier to 6 in. wide.

Votives

Votive candleholders are little containers used for burning small candles. Originally used for religious purposes, they also make lovely contemporary decorations and can be embellished in a variety of ways.

Votive candleholders can be made from many different materials: brass, wood, pottery, and glass, to name just a few. The technique demonstrated here shows how to cover a glass votive with polymer clay. You can buy glass votives in various sizes, but an ordinary glass tumbler will work just as well.

Polymer clay, or oven-baked modeling clay, is available in a wonderful range of colors including translucent. It is an ideal material for decorating small glass votives—if you use translucent clay, the candlelight shines through to make a rich and colorful glow. If the clay is stiff, knead it for a few minutes before use until it is soft and smooth. To mix the colors, simply press together the required quantities and roll and fold repeatedly until the streaks have disappeared and a new color is formed.

The technique used here is called "caning" and involves making logs of clay that have a pattern running all through their length. It is possible to buy ready-made canes of polymer clay to apply to votives if you prefer.

☞
**Stained Glass Candles,
pages 106-108**

YOU WILL NEED

Polymer clay—black, crimson, yellow, blue, turquoise green, translucent
Smooth board or work surface
Two thin strips of wood or card, 1/16 in. thick
Smooth bottle or rolling pin
Craft knife
Drinking glass
PVA glue and glue spreader
Baking tray, lined with cookie sheets or paper

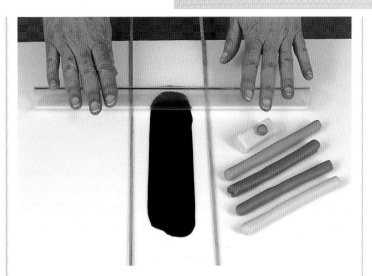

1 Mix the polymer clay to make a translucent mixture with the blue, yellow, pink, and turquoise clays by adding one part color to about 20 parts of translucent clay. You will need about 1/2 oz. of each color. Roll out some black clay between the wood strips to make a sheet of even thickness.

2 Form the yellow translucent clay mixture into a log, about 3/8 in. thick and 6 in. long. Wrap it in the black sheet, butting the edges for a neat fit, to make a simple bull's-eye cane. Repeat to produce wrapped logs of the other translucent clay mixtures.

3 Cut the blue cane into three equal lengths and lay them on the board. Place two yellow canes, cut to the same length, on top into the dips between the blue canes. Don't worry if they are not completely round, but keep them the same diameter.

4 | Squeeze the canes together, and roll the resulting log back and forth on the board. Press down lightly with your hands while moving them up and down the length of the log so that the log reduces in thickness evenly and lengthens. Keep rolling until the new cane is about ½ in. thick.

5 | Lay the cane on your board with the yellow parts at the top. Pinch all along the length of the cane to form it into a triangle cross-section. Cut it into six equal lengths. Stack three of these together, yellow points to the center, to make a semicircular cross-section, pressing them together on the work surface to consolidate.

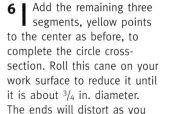

6 | Add the remaining three segments, yellow points to the center as before, to complete the circle cross-section. Roll this cane on your work surface to reduce it until it is about ¾ in. diameter. The ends will distort as you roll but when you cut the cane in half, the pattern will be there, running right through the cane, a smaller version of the original. Cut a 4 in. length of this cane.

7 | Take the pink and turquoise bulls-eye canes and press them together in pairs. Roll to reduce to about ½ in. diameter and shape into a triangular cross-section as before. Cut this cane into four 4 in. lengths, and press them on the first cane, with the points facing outwards.

8 | This cane cannot be rolled to reduce or the square section will be distorted. Hold it vertically in one hand and stroke downward with the other, pulling it to lengthen and reduce it. Rotate the cane after every few pulls and keep inverting it to keep both ends even. Again, the last inch or so at each end will distort but the pattern will remain perfect in the center.

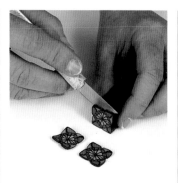

9 | When the cane is about ¾ in. across, leave it to rest for about 30 minutes. Take a sharp knife or blade and trim off the end. Cut very thin slices from the cane, rotating the cane a quarter turn after each cut to minimize distortion.

10 | Apply a thin coat of PVA glue to the bottom half of the glass. This will provide a key for the clay when you press it on the glass. It does not matter if the glue dries while you work as it will still provide a key.

11 | Roll out a strip of black clay, trim the edges neatly, and press it on the base of the glass, butting the ends together. Press on the cane slices, slightly overlapping the black strip and each previous slice. Work around the glass in rows, leaving a gap between each slice for the light to shine through. You can reduce a length of the cane further to make smaller slices for the narrower parts of the glass.

▼ Place a small votive candle or a tea light inside the votive holder. The pink votive in the picture has been made in the same way, but the polymer clay cane slices were butted together to form a continuous covering.

12 | Work all the way up to the top of the glass, applying more glue as necessary. When the glass is covered, place it on a baking sheet and bake for 30 minutes at 265°F, or follow the clay manufacturers' instructions. When the glass has cooled, you can remove traces of glue visible in the spaces between the canes by immersing the glass in water and scrubbing the glue away with a toothbrush.

Displaying Candles

Choosing suitable holders and
containers for your candles is great
fun, and the variety available
is enormous. But don't
restrict yourself to commercial
candleholders—unusual and
unexpected artifacts can also be
highly effective.

On the left of the picture is a collection of chrome
and brass candlesticks that would suit many
decorative situations owing to their simplicity.
These holders can be left plain or decorated with
candle cuffs or flower arrangements. Above is a
terra-cotta wall sconce. The hanging hurricane
lantern holds a tea light and will burn safely for
hours. Below is a candleholder with glass bowls for
burning small votives or tea lights. Pillar candles
are easy to display because they are so stable, and
a wooden cutlery box makes an unusual holder. To
the right of this, a glass candle shade adds a
touch of sophistication. A metal device fits over the
candle and keeps the shade above the flame as
the candle burns down. Three glass night-lights on
the mantelpiece show how a tea light or votive can
be transformed into a small lamp, unencumbered
by a trailing wire.

GALLERY

When you enjoy making and decorating candles, it is always fascinating to see the work of other candlemakers, particularly those who have honed their craft to an inspirational level. The Gallery that follows contains candles by many innovative and experienced candlemakers and provides a glittering feast for the eye.

Dipping and Beyond

Dipping is the traditional method of making candles that produces the elegant lines of the familiar taper. Dipping can also be used to embellish candles in a variety of ways, from the simple to the extraordinary.

The rainbow of hand-dipped tapers by master candlemaker Inger John, at the top of the picture, shows candles hung in pairs in the traditional way. Several have been given a graded overdip so that their colors change gradually from the bottom to the top. The exotic whirls of the two water candles on the left aptly resemble fantastic images from an underwater scene. These candles are formed by plunging tapers into cold water while molten wax is poured around them. The next four are incised candles, which are made by overdipping a molded candle and then cutting or carving into the wax coating to reveal the color below. The four candles on the far right, with another pair hanging above, are "dip and carve" candles: a molded core is dipped many times into wax to build up several layers of contrasting color. The candle is then carved to create flaps, which are twisted and curled into exotic shapes.

Molding for Symmetry

Rigid molds provide the means of creating candles in a glorious variety of symmetrical shapes. There are many ingenious ways to vary these simple forms with color, inclusions, and layered pouring.

The three "net" candles on the left of the picture are from Denmark. When these candles burn down, a tracery of wax lace is left behind. Next are three landscape candles, which are built up with layers of different colored wax to suggest landscapes, while the "trees" are pressed ferns. To the right of these is a selection of candles with wax chunk inclusions. Some of the chunks are molded shapes which combine with the vivid colors of the wax to suggest mystical images within the candles. To the right of the candle with the blue figures is a purple pillar candle with wax paint inclusions. On the far right are several ice candles, made by filling a mold with crushed ice and then pouring in the wax. The ice melts to give an eccentric pattern of holes within the molded shape of the candle.

Ornamental Candles

There are innumerable ways in which candles are created and decorated. They can be hand-shaped or modeled, cast in molds, painted, wrapped, gilded, or hammered—the list is almost endless.

The picture demonstrates the extraordinary variety of ornamental candles. At the top left are a group of stained-glass candles that are created using millefiori wax. The three small fish at the top center are hand-modeled with modeling wax. At the top right are several candles cast from original sculptures, including three in the shape of dragons emerging from eggs. The marbled pink and green table napkin candle in the center, and the yellow candle below right, are both hand-formed. The silver candle at the bottom left, and the purple candle above it, have been decorated by hammering the candle surface while the wax was still soft. Above the purple candle, a lilac candle is wrapped with hand-made paper, lace, and ribbons. At the center bottom are two white appliquéd candles decorated with ivy leaves, and blue and gold squares, respectively.

Naturals

Nature is a rich source of inspiration for many crafts, especially in candle-making where the simple elements of wax and flame are beautifully enhanced by a natural theme.

Clockwise from the left foreground: Three molded fruit candles are scented with appropriate fruit scents. Behind them are two sweet-pepper candles that were molded in the vegetables to give a glorious surface texture. Behind and to the right of these is a gel candle; a wick is inserted into a tumbler of transparent gel wax in which seashells and pebbles are immersed. Behind are a pillar candle wrapped with ears of wheat, and a candle decorated with a multitude of seashells. The tall pyramid candle is made using beeswax sheets, and the two scalloped candles are molded in the scooped-out shells of acorn squashes. Several inclusions candles follow containing pebbles, seashells, flowers, and herbs. Toward the bottom right are two simple container candles in oyster shells, followed by three sand candles. Finally, two coconut candles use coconut shells lined with gold leaf as containers.

Floating Candles

Water and flame is a glorious combination and floating candles use both elements to create a glow of shimmering light on water. These little candles will burn for a surprisingly long time.

The picture shows a sparkling collection of floating candles displayed in glass containers with flowers, petals, and glass pebbles. Matching color and form gives particularly appealing results: In the left foreground, a collection of yellow star candles float with tiny narcissi in a glass bowl; the stars mirror the shapes of the flowers and the painted decoration on the bowl. Several small bowls each hold a single floating candle—a charming centerpiece on a table for two. The central blue bowl contains several "oil-on-water" candles: These are shaped plastic disks that hold a wick and are floated on a thin layer of vegetable oil on the surface of the water. The wick burns by drawing up the oil, and if the disk is clear plastic, it gives the impression of a flame issuing from the water itself. Some of the disks are colored and in the shape of delicate flowers.

Further Reading

Gary V. Guy, *Easy-to-Make Candles*,
Dover Publications 1979
*Slim but useful book on the main techniques
of candlemaking*

David Constable, *Candlemaking*,
Search Press 1992
*Basic candlemaking with some more
advanced techniques*

Gloria Nicol, *The New Candle Book*,
Lorenz Books 1995
*Many inspirational photographs for
displaying candles as well as projects.*

Sue Spear, *Creative Candles*,
Greenwich Editions 1996
Mainly a project book.

Miranda Innes, *The Book of Candles*,
Dorling Kindersley 1987
*An inspiring display book of different types
of candle. Basic candlemaking instructions.*

Chris Larkin, *The Book of Candlemaking*,
Sterling Publishing 1998
*Many new and original ideas for making
and decorating candles.*

Candlemaking Suppliers

AUSTRALIA

Candles Plus
Shop #18, Hill Top Shopping Centre
O'Halloran Hill
South Australia
Tel: (08) 8322 8766
email: vidb@ozemail.com.au
website:
http://www.ausdiscount.com.au/candles.htm

*Shop selling a wide range of candles – also
candlemaking supplies and mail order.*

Redpath's Beekeeping Supplies
193 Como Parade East
Parkdale, Vic 3195
Australia
Tel and Fax: (03) 9587 5950
website:
http://www.contact.com.au/beehive/

Beeswax and molds by mail order

CANADA

Lynden House International Inc.
12605A–127 Avenue
Edmonton
Alberta
T5L 3E8
Tel: (403) 448 1994
Toll Free Number: 1-877-6CRAFTS (Valid
                             Canada-Wide)
Fax: (403) 448-0086
website:
http://www.compusmart.ab.ca/sbra/lynden/

Candlemaking supplies by mail order

Ashburnham Craft Supplies
120 Hunter St. E.
Peterborough
Ontario
K9H 1G6
Tel: (705) 742 6083
Fax: (705) 742 3005
email: ashburnham@sympatico.ca
website:
http://www3.sympatico.ca/ashburnham/

*General crafts and candlemaking supplies.
Store and mail order*

NEW ZEALAND

Golding Handcrafts
PO Box 9022
Wellington
Tel /Fax: (04) 384 9347
email: epdyne@compuserve.com
http://www.goldingcraft.com

*General crafts and candlemaking supplies.
Stores and mail order*

USA

Candles and More
75-10 Rockaway Boulevard
PO Box 211186
Woodhaven, New York 11421
Tel: (516) 248 8102
website:
http://www.craftcave.com/candle/canhome
.htm

*Candlemaking supplies and equipment by
mail order*

Glorybee Candlemaking Supplies
PO Box 2744
Eugene, OR 97402
Tel: 1 (800) GLORYBE (456-7923).
Fax: (541) 689 9692
email: sales@glorybee.com
website: http://www.glorybee.com

*Beeswax and candlemaking supplies, store
and mail order*

Pourette Candle Making Supplies
1418 NW 53rd St
Seattle, WA 98107-3737
Tel: (206) 789 3188
website: http://www.pourette.com

*Candlemaking supplies and equipment, mold
manufacturer. Store and mail order.*

The Wax House
239 Market Ave
Waynesboro, VA. 22980
Tel: Toll Free (US and Canada)
    888-WAX-9711
Fax: Toll Free (US and Canada) 877-
    WAX-9711
International Orders Tel: 540-949-7300
website: http:// www.waxhouse.com

*Candlemaking supplies and equipment by
mail order*

UK

The Candles Shop
30 The Market
Covent Garden
London WC2E 8RE
Tel: (0) 171 836 9815
Fax: (0) 171 240 8065

*Candles, candleholders and candlemaking
supplies*

Candle Makers Supplies
28 Blythe Road
LondonW14 OHA
Tel: (0) 171 602 4031/2
Fax: (0) 171 602 2796

Shop and mail order candlemaking supplies

Poth Hille
37 High Street
Stratford
London E15 2QD
Tel: (0) 181 534 7091
Fax: (0) 181 534 2291

Wholesale suppliers of wax

E.H. Thornes Ltd
Beehive Works
Wragby
Lincoln LN3 5LA
Tel: (0) 1673 858555
Fax: (0) 1673 857004
email: thorne@dial.pipex.com
website: http://www.thorne.co.uk

*Mail order beeswax and candlemaking
supplies*

WEBSITES

Candle and Soap Mining Company:
http://candleandsoap.miningco.com/

*A large site full of projects, resources and
useful links*

Candle Makers:
http://users.wantree.com.au/~campbell/c
andles.htm

*An Australian based site full of
candlemaking advice and links*

http://www.craftcave.com/candle/canindex
.shtml

Inspirational candles and candle supplies

Index

SSD in parentheses following a page number indicates a step-by-step demonstration.
Page numbers in **bold** type refers to an illustration in the gallery.

Credits

Quarto Publishing would like to thank the following :

The candlemakers who demonstrated the candlemaking:

David Coffey: pages 60-3, 74-5, 82-3
Inger John: pages 28-33, 50-3, 56-9, 66-71, 96-7, 104-5
Judith Scales: pages 26-7, 34-5, 38-45, 48-9, 112-15
Irene Worsdell: pages 22-5
The remained techniques were demonstrated by the author.

The candlemakers who loaned candles for the gallery:

ananas & dansk (Import, Export, Wholesale, Retail), Camp Road, Lowestoft, Suffolk, NR32 2LL, United Kingdom. Tel: (0)1502 514848 Fax (0)1502 514828 Website: http://www.ananas.co.uk

The Candlemaker, Mill Road, Stokesby, Gt. Yarmouth, Norfolk NR29 3EY, United Kingdom. Tel/Fax (0)1493 750242.

Clearlight Candles, London House, Lynn Road, Gayton, Kings Lynn PE32 1QJ, United Kingdom. Tel: (0)1553 636430 Website: http://www.clearlightcandles.co.uk

David Coffey, Candelight Gifts, Stowmarket, Suffolk IP14 4QS, United Kingdom.

David Constable of Candle Makers Supplies, 28 Blythe Rd, London W14 OHA, United Kingdom.

Craftplan, Unit 89, Woodside Business Park, Shore Road, Birkenhead, Merseyside L41 1E, United Kingdom.

Suzanne Gray Original Handpainted Glass, 65A Beresford Road, London N5 2HR, United Kingdom, e-mail: sujiro.gray@btinternet.com

David and Doreen Grigor, 28 Cornflower Rd, Haydon Wick, Swindon, Wilts SN2 3SA, United Kingdom. Tel: (0)1793 727320.

Inger John, Pembrokeshire Candle Centre, Trefelin, Cilgwyn, Newport, Pembrokeshire SA42 0QN, United Kingdom. Tel: (0)1239 820470.

Lily-Flame Candles, 67 Chippenham Road, Maida Vale, London W9 2AB, United Kingdom. Tel: (0)171 2661995.

Local Crafts Dolgellau, Bridge Street, Dolgellau, Gwynedd LL40 2AU, United Kingdom.

Marinus K. engros A/S, Postbox 324, Strømøvej 3, DK-Horsens, Denmark.

Peter W. Neuman, Unit 2, Will Farm Workshops, Colston Road, Buckfastleigh, Devon TQ11 0LW, United Kingdom.

P. Peterson Ltd, 21 Southey Street, Penge, London SE20 7JD, United Kingdom.

Judith Scales, The Norfolk Candle Company. Phone/fax (0)1502 677 313

Stoneglow Candles, Selinas Lane, Dagenham, Essex RM8 1QH, United Kingdom. Tel: (0)181 5958878.

Too Good to Burn Company, 28 Excelsior Street, Widcombe, Bath, BA2 4JB, United Kingdom. Tel: (0)1225 310312.

Wang's International Ltd, Cae Maur Industrial Estate, Treorchy, Rhondda, Mid-Glamorgan, CF42 6EJ, United Kingdom.

Waxworks, Bernard and Isabel Pearson, Windy Ridge Studios, Woolpit, Suffolk IP30 9SH, United Kingdom. Phone: (0)1359 240927 Fax (0)1359 244036 e-mail: HYPERLINK mailto: Isobel@behemoth.demon.co.uk Isobel@behemoth.demon.co.uk.

Irene Worsdell, Handcarved Candle Company, 1 Foundry House, Hall St, Long Melford, Sudbury, Suffolk CO10 9JR, United Kingdom. Tel: (0)1787 313342.

The candlemaking companies who loaned equipment and materials:

E.H.Thorne (Beehives) Ltd Beehive Works, Wragby, Market Rasen, Lincs LN8 5LA, United Kingdom. e-mail: thorne@dial.pipex.com; website http://www.thorne.co.uk

The Candle Shop, 50 New Kings Road, London SW6 4LS. Also at 39 The Market, London WC2E 8RE, United Kingdom

Edding (UK) Ltd, Marabu Glass Art Materials, Merlin Centre, Acrewood Way, St Albans, Herts AL4 0JY, United Kingdom. Tel: (0)1727 846688 Fax: (0)1727 839970